PEOPLES *of*

NORTH AMERICA

VOLUME 6

Iroquois Confederacy – Local politics, Canada

About This Book

Peoples of North America is a survey of the North American population at the start of the 21st century: the ethnic groups who make it up, their origins, culture, and lifestyle. The 10 volumes of the encyclopedia are organized alphabetically and describe all ethnic groups, from Afghans to West Africans. The peoples include well-established communities, relatively recent immigrants, and indigenous peoples who survive in significant numbers. Other entries also cover immigration-related and crosscultural subjects, such as inter-marriage, music, and race, to help you understand how different groups have contributed to shaping modern North America.

Each entry on a specific ethnic group explains who the people are and where they live, where they came from, how they lived in the past and how they live now, and their arts, culture, and politics. Fact files and maps show the states and cities where the major com-munities live today. The fact files also allow you to quickly find useful information, including population figures, immigration history, languages, dominant religions, typical jobs, national foods, typical names, famous individuals, and major community organiz-ations. The statistical data are from the U.S. and Canadian censuses. Where no date is specified, the data are based on the latest available figures: the 2000 U.S. Census or the 1996 Canadian Census.

Entries on ethnic groups all contain a box listing useful websites. There are also special boxes giving detailed information about key people, events, places, cultures, or traditions. A "See also" box at the end of each entry points you to related articles elsewhere in the encyclopedia, allowing you to further investigate topics of interest.

The index covers all 10 volumes, so it will help you trace topics throughout the set. A glossary at the end of each book gives a brief explanation of important words and concepts, and a timeline provides a chronological account of key events in the history of immigration to North America.

First Published 2003 by Grolier,
an imprint of Scholastic Library Publishing,
Old Sherman Turnpike
Danbury, Connecticut 06816

© 2003 The Brown Reference Group plc

Set ISBN: 0–7172–5777–0
Volume 6 ISBN: 0–7172–5783–5

Library of Congress Cataloging-in-Publication Data

Peoples of North America
      p. cm.
   Includes indexes
   Summary: Profiles the native and immigrant groups that have peopled North America, focusing on the modes and monitoring of immigration.
   Contents: v. 1. Afghans-Bosnians – v. 2. Brazilians-Colombians – v. 3. Colonial America-Egyptians – v. 4. Emigrés and refugees-Guyanese – v. 5. Gypsies (Romany)-Irish – v. 6. Iroquois confederacy-local politics, Canda – v. 7. Local politics, U.S.-Native Americans, Southeast – v. 8. Native Americans, Southwest and Mexico-Puerto Ricans – v. 9. Quebec separatism-social mobility and race – v. 10. South Africans-World War II.
   ISBN 0-7172-5777-0 (set : alk. paper)
   1. Minorities – North America – Encyclopedias, Juvenile. 2. Immigrants – North America – Encyclopedias, Juvenile. 3. Ethnology – North America – Encyclopedias, Juvenile. 4. North America – Population – Encyclopedias, Juvenile. 5. North America – History – Encyclopedias, Juvenile. 6. North America – Ethnic relations – Encyclopedias, Juvenile. [1. North America – Population – Encyclopedias. 2. Ethnology – North America – Encyclopedias.]

E49.P467 2003
305.8'0097'03 – dc21

                                        2003042395

For information address the publisher:
Grolier, Scholastic Library Publishing,
Old Sherman Turnpike, Danbury, Connecticut 06816

Printed and bound in Singapore

For The Brown Reference Group plc
Academic Consultants: Donald Avery, Professor, Department of History, University of Western Ontario;
Margaret Connell-Szasz, Professor of Native American and Celtic History, University of New Mexico
Editors: Rachel Bean, Andrew Campbell, Dennis Cove, Felicity Crowe, Mark Fletcher, Lee Stacy
Designer: Dax Fullbrook
Picture Researcher: Becky Cox
Indexer: Kay Ollerenshaw
Managing Editor: Tim Cooke

CONTENTS

Iroquois Confederacy	4
Israelis	8
Italians	10
Jamaicans	17
Japanese	20
Jews	25
Jordanians	32
Koreans	33
Kurds	37
Kuwaitis	38
Labor unions	39
Language retention	41
Laotians	46
Latvians	48
Lebanese	50
Liberians	52
Linguistic groups	54
Literacy	59
Literature	62
Lithuanians	66
Local politics, Canada	68
Glossary	70
Further reading	71
Immigration timeline	72
Set index	73

Iroquois Confederacy

Useful websites

About the Iroquois Confederacy (www.factmonster.com/ce6/society/A0825512.html)

Background to the Iroquois Nations (www.crystalinks.com/iroquois.html)

Constitution of the Iroquois Nations (www.constitution.org/cons/iroquois.htm)

Iroquois Confederacy and the U.S. Constitution (www.iroquois democracy.pdx.edu)

Iroquois.net (www.iroquois.net)

Iroquois stories (www.indians.org/welker/iroqoral.htm)

The Iroquois Confederacy was founded between 1450 and 1525 and included five distinct Native American tribes, or "nations": Cayuga, Mohawk, Oneida, Onondaga, and Seneca. In the 1720s the Tuscarora tribe joined, and the confederacy then became known as the Six Nations. Traditionally, these Native Americans inhabited an extensive portion of the northeastern area that became New England and an eastern portion of what is now Canada. A majority of Iroquoian descendants continue to occupy some of the original ancestral homelands, for example, living on designated reservations. Some Iroquois do not completely acknowledge the national boundaries of the United States and Canada, since many retain an Iroquoian identity regardless of the country in which they now reside.

Their traditional collective name is "Haudenosaunee," meaning "People Building the Long House" or "People of the Long House." A long house was the traditional dwelling in which several family groups would live together. After contact with early European settlers the names of the Native Americans were often altered. However, the vast majority of modern Iroquois still to refer to themselves collectively as Haudenosaunee, as well as by their respective nations.

Iroquois Identity

The Iroquois are connected through ancient kinship relationships. Both in traditional and contemporary societies these relationships provide opportunities for individuals, their immediate and extended families or "clans," and their tribes to uphold and enact toward one another the duties that have created and support the foundations of Haudenosaunee culture. Iroquois group identity reflects ways of life, laws, core beliefs, social organizations, and the responsibilities of all groups within the confederacy. These common sets of values include a democratic system of government.

According to Haudenosaunee traditions, clans were named for nine animals: bear, deer, wolf, beaver, eel, turtle, hawk, heron, and snipe. Clan members are related to and are responsible for each other, and marriages within a clan are forbidden. This system of clan identity remains intact and is of great importance.

Clan Mothers and Hoyaneh

In the Iroquois culture ancestry is traced through the mother's line. Iroquois women hold an influential social, spiritual, and political position and are responsible for the well-being of their

An Iroquois man dances and chants in the snow outside a reconstruction of a traditional Iroquois long house.

clans. Traditionally, women have been the decision-makers on issues such as whether to wage war. They are also the property owners, and all rights of inheritance are transmitted through the maternal lineage.

The eldest females are "clan mothers" who are responsible for naming and counseling their respective clan members, as well as arranging marriages and monitoring clan behavior. Clan mother titles are hereditary, and it is the elder sisters and eldest daughters who determine the next woman most worthy of becoming the clan mother.

Clan mothers, with the general consensus of the clan, nominate, approve, and install "hoyaneh," the male leaders or chiefs. Hoyaneh are the visible representatives in the political arena and are generally assigned to office for life but can be removed from office for violating any laws. Hoyaneh are required to look out for the welfare of all of the people, be honest, fair, and trustworthy, and be knowledgeable of and uphold all Haudenosaunee laws. Accordingly, the male leaders serve as representatives of their respective clans to the Grand Council of the Haudenosaunee. Clans have more than one hoyaneh, and all hoyaneh have equal say, equal power, and equal authority.

Iroquois social structure

Iroquois society can be seen as having several interconnecting concentric circles. An Iroquois individual is at the center of his or her circle and is a member of the immediate family. Through lineage he or she is also joined to other extended family units, or "clan." Clans are encircled by membership in a respective nation—Cayuga, Mohawk, Oneida, Onondaga, Seneca, or Tuscarora. The outermost circle then joins all Six Nations into the Iroquois Confederacy as a whole.

Fact File: IROQUOIS CONFEDERACY

Region of origin

WISCONSIN
VERMONT
NEW HAMPSHIRE
OKLAHOMA
OHIO
PENNSYLVANIA
NEW YORK

Population

United States: approximately 42,300 (early 1990s); Canada: approximately 25,600 (early 1990s).

Festivals

Midwinter, Thanks-to-the-Maple, Corn Planting, Strawberry, Green Corn, and Harvest festivals.

Food

Mainly corn eaten baked, boiled, on or off the cob, or sweetened with maple sap. Also squash, game, and fish.

Jobs

Originally farmers, now ironworkers (Mohawks), factory or domestic workers, or in health and education.

Language groups

Iroquois dialects: Onondaga, Mohawk, Oneida, Cayuga, Seneca, and Tuscarora.

Notable Iroquois individual

Onondaga Chief Oren Lyons (1930–) has been a political leader, successful lacrosse goalkeeper, amateur boxer, commercial artist, author and illustrator, and publisher of a Native American quarterly newspaper.

This image dates from around 1900 and shows an Iroquois family outside a tepee. They are wearing the traditional dress of their tribe.

The Grand Council

The 50-member Grand Council is a self-governing organization based on principles of "peace, power, and righteousness." It resembles a two-house body with an effective system of checks and balances. A general consensus among all 50 hoyaneh must be achieved before agreement is reached and action taken. Some modern communities also have elected officials who function similarly to non-Indian government officials, but the traditional council is independent of them and continues to function according to its own laws.

The Grand Council works together on all matters that concern the Haudenosaunee. Generally, an issue is presented first to the Mohawk and Seneca councils for discussion and then to the Cayuga and Oneida councils. Matters are then handed on to the Onondaga Council, which is responsible for recording meetings and making any final ratifications.

Iroquois and the Early Settlers

Early European settlers adopted several Iroquois practices in order to survive in the newly colonized lands, including many ideas that characterized Iroquois democracy. During the 18th century a number of colonial leaders witnessed and admired the Iroquois Confederacy in action. One such leader was Benjamin Franklin who spent a significant time among the Iroquois making notes about their distinctive cultural characteristics and the effectiveness of their established systems of governance. As a result, some of the Iroquois concepts of governing may have been adapted by the framers of the Constitution when it was drafted in Philadelphia in 1787.

As a result of the relations between the Iroquois and the early colonists, a unique bond developed between the Iroquoian peoples and the federal government. Historical treaties were drawn up between the two parties and usually dealt with land ownership. They continue to be legally binding agreements that affect contemporary society and issues between indigenous and nonindigenous peoples.

Similarly, the Iroquois were influenced by the arrival of the Europeans and adopted several aspects of their culture. Although many remained resistant to European religious teachings, a large number of Iroquois converted to Christianity. Long-house religion has remained for many, particularly the Onondaga and Seneca, the only form of spiritual practice. However, it is not unusual to find Iroquois practicing Christianity and their indigenous religion in tandem.

As the Iroquois began to trade with Europeans, their own traditions started to change. Large areas of their once vast land were traded for useful Western goods or taken by the federal governments. The reduction in their lands made hunting for food and skins more difficult, and gradually men moved into agricultural work, an area formerly dominated by women. This change in turn brought about the end of communal living as families left the long houses to live on the land on small farms.

Iroquois-owned territory shrank immeasurably in the 19th century, due, in part, to European trade, but also to the implementation of various land acts that took land from the Iroquois. As a result, the Iroquois were forced onto reservations in just a small portion of their original territory. Today, however, they are more spread out, and there are 17 Iroquois communities in North America, including parts of New York, Wisconsin, and Oklahoma in the United States and Quebec and Toronto in Canada.

This scene in Montreal, Canada, shows a group of Mohawks drumming outside the Berri-UQAM subway station in a display of traditional Mohawk singing and dancing.

Contemporary Iroquois

Many longstanding Iroquois ways of life, values, and traditional laws have been passed down from one generation to the next. Now, as in the past, the Iroquois are not fully assimilated into mainstream American and Canadian culture. Haudenosaunee cultures have continuously been maintained to sustain their distinctiveness.

However, despite shunning total assimilation, modern Iroquois can be found in many areas of employment. Mohawk men are famous as ironworkers. They are also renowned for their skills in high-rise construction and have worked on the building of some of America's most famous landmarks, such as the Empire State Building, the Chrysler Building, and the Golden Gate Bridge. Other Iroquois have found employment as factory or domestic workers and in the healthcare and education sectors.

Today some Iroquois live outside the traditional homeland, but their familial connections often remain intact. The vast majority of modern Iroquoian peoples live contemporary lifestyles while preserving traditional practices and values. An example of this cultural continuity includes their consideration of the effect on at least seven future generations of any decisions being made today.

Most Iroquois are strongly committed to maintaining their culture. Both individually and collectively, the Haudenosaunee believe compliance with their personal, cultural, and spiritual duties will provide cultural stability. And clan mothers and hoyaneh continue to be socially, spiritually, and politically responsible for their communities, clans, nations, and all other members of the confederacy.

See also

- Native Americans (Volumes 7 & 8)
- Native American workers (Volume 8)
- Reservation system (Volume 9)

About 75,000 people crowded into Madison Square in New York on May 17, 1948, to support the new Jewish state on the day that Israel declared its independence.

The state of Israel lies in the Middle East and is bordered by Lebanon, Syria, Jordan, Egypt, and the Mediterranean. Israel was established in 1948 as a Jewish state, following the mass extermination of Jews in Europe by the German Nazis in the 1930s and 1940s. It was founded as a democratic country where Jews from all over the world could come and live. Israel's population was largely made up of Jewish immigrants who came from Western and Central Europe, the United States, Russia (formerly part of the Soviet Union), and North Africa. However, not all Israelis are Jewish. Palestine, where Israel is located, is also the home to other ethnic groups—Muslim Arabs, Christian Arabs, and Druze (a separate Arabic-speaking community). In 2002 the total population of Israel was over 6.5 million, of which about one-sixth is Arab and four-fifths Jewish.

Israeli American Population

It is very difficult to know how many Jewish Israelis have immigrated to the United States because there are no reliable statistics. The term "Israeli" indicates that a person was born within the borders of the state of Israel, so Israeli immigrant statistics can include both Arabs and Jews. For example, by 1990 an estimated 15,000 Palestinian Arabs had migrated to the United States as Israelis. In addition, Israel does not compile statistics on emigrants from its country, and the Israeli American community is a mixture of both documented and undocumented immigrants—many visit relatives and then remain.

Research in the late 1980s by a sociologist and Israeli emigré, Pini Herman, estimated that there were 116,000 Israeli-born Jews living in the United States in 1988 and 120,000 in 1991. Today the total Israeli American community is estimated at between 110,000 to 135,000. An estimated 30,000 to 56,000 Jewish immigrants from Israel, but not Israeli born, have entered the United States as "Israelis." About 42,000 Israeli Americans are second generation.

Waves of Immigration

The first wave of immigration was the result of Jewish families reuniting in the United States after the European upheavals of the mid-20th century, as well as people deciding that life in Israel was too austere—much of Israel is desert. Wars with Israel's neighbors—the Six-Day War (1967) and the Yom Kippur War (1973)—and high taxation caused a second wave of immigration that lasted through the 1980s. It is estimated that between 100,000 and 400,000 Israelis immigrated during this second wave. Emigration slowed in the early 1990s due to increased economic growth in Israel and a simultaneous economic slump in California, where many Israelis had settled. In the mid- to late 1990s immigration increased again. This time it was mainly in response to the ongoing uprisings, known as the Intifadah, by Palestinians who live in the Israeli-occupied territories of the West Bank and Gaza Strip. Since the Intifadah started in 1987, over 2,000 Palestinians and 500 Israelis have been killed. For some Israelis the United States seems to offer better educational and career opportunities, a more secure society, and less anti-Jewish sentiment.

Most Israeli immigrants have settled among the large Jewish populations of New York and Los Angeles. Most are well educated and affluent, and fewer than 4 percent are employed as blue-collar workers (manual laborers). Individual Israelis have successfully become involved in American culture, especially in the fields of music and art. Israeli Americans have established Hebrew newspapers and journals, as well as Hebrew radio stations. Some Israeli Americans speak Hebrew in their homes. As a group, their connections to Israel remain strong, and most travel to Israel regularly to visit relatives.

Israeli American foods include the Middle Eastern specialities of falafel and hummus, which have become readily available in the United States. Their folk dancing also continues to be popular among Jewish Americans.

Notable Israeli Americans

Itzhak Perlman, violinist.
Ariella Shamir, artist.
Gene Simmons, bass player for
   the rock band KISS.
Pinchas Zukerman, violinist.

See also

• Arab Americans (Volume 1)
• Jews (Volume 6)
• Jordanians (Volume 6)
• Palestinians (Volume 8)

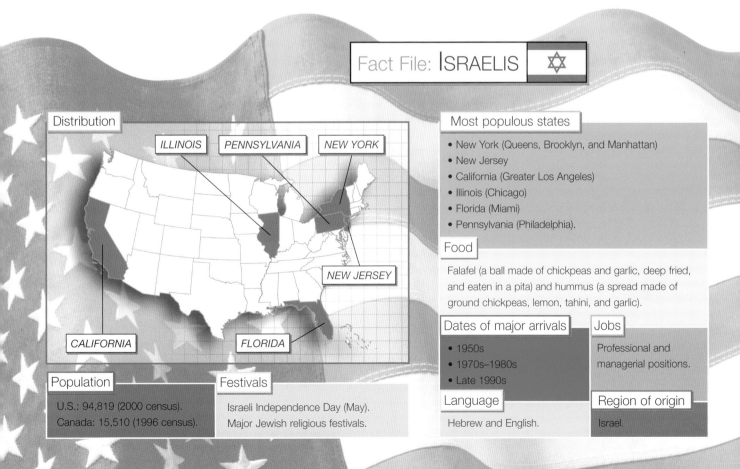

Fact File: ISRAELIS ✡

Distribution

ILLINOIS   PENNSYLVANIA   NEW YORK

NEW JERSEY

CALIFORNIA   FLORIDA

Most populous states

• New York (Queens, Brooklyn, and Manhattan)
• New Jersey
• California (Greater Los Angeles)
• Illinois (Chicago)
• Florida (Miami)
• Pennsylvania (Philadelphia).

Food

Falafel (a ball made of chickpeas and garlic, deep fried, and eaten in a pita) and hummus (a spread made of ground chickpeas, lemon, tahini, and garlic).

Dates of major arrivals

• 1950s
• 1970s–1980s
• Late 1990s

Jobs

Professional and managerial positions.

Language

Hebrew and English.

Region of origin

Israel.

Population

U.S.: 94,819 (2000 census).
Canada: 15,510 (1996 census).

Festivals

Israeli Independence Day (May).
Major Jewish religious festivals.

Useful websites

The Italian Historical Society of
America (www.italianhistorical.org)
The National Italian American
Foundation (www.niaf.org)
When Italian Americans were
"enemy aliens"
(www.io.com/~segreta)
Italian language
(http://italian.about.com)
Italian culture
(www.virtualitalia.com)

A group of Italian immigrants attending a class on English language and U.S. citizenship in the 1920s. The Department of Labor organized classes such as this to help new immigrants assimilate into American life.

While Italian Americans remain a distinct social and cultural group, large numbers of them have entered the American cultural mainstream. Today more than 15 million Americans (6 percent of the population) acknowledge Italian ancestry, although 26 million (10.5 percent of the American population) have at least one ancestor from Italy. Most self-identified Italian Americans live in the northeastern United States—7.5 million in New York, New Jersey, Pennsylvania, Massachusetts, and Connecticut alone.

Like their cousins in Italy, Italian Americans have tended to live close to their places of birth, so most reside in the Northeast. Over the past 40 years, however, two trends have developed. Significant numbers of Italian Americans have moved from urban ethnic enclaves, or "Little Italies," to nearby suburban towns. Prior to World War II (1939–1945), for example, nearly all Italian Americans in the state of New York lived in its cities. Since then, so many have left for the suburbs that as of 1990, they made up anywhere from 12 to 28 percent of the population of counties surrounding cities. Italian Americans' economic success and resettlement in the suburbs have led to a great deal of cultural assimilation. At the same time, many Italian Americans have moved from the Northeast to warmer, less urban areas of the country, especially Florida (800,000 Italian Americans), Arizona (160,000), and California (1.5 million), the last of which already had a significant Italian American population dating from the late 19th century.

In Canada over one million people have Italian ancestry. The majority of Italian immigrants in Canada originally settled in the cities in the northeast, where they developed "Little Italies." By 1981 over 87 percent of all Italian Canadians were living in Ontario or Quebec, the majority in Toronto and Montreal. Today there are also Italian communities in Calgary, Edmonton, and Vancouver.

The Great Wave of Immigration

Before 1860 fewer than 100,000 Italians lived in North America. In that year Giuseppe Garibaldi and 1,000 loyal troops in the service of the fledgling Italian Republic liberated southern Italy from the oppressive rule of the Bourbon monarchs. The Bourbons were French and Spanish kings who centuries earlier had conquered the many principalities that shared the southern half of the Italian peninsula. In doing so, they established the Kingdom of the Two Sicilies. The Bourbon monarchs ruled over a government that exploited the

Distribution

Most populous states: New York, New Jersey, California, Pennsylvania, Massachusetts, Florida, Illinois, Ohio, Connecticut, Michigan.

Most populous cities: New York City; Philadelphia, Pennsylvania; Chicago, Illinois; Boston, Massachusetts; Pittsburgh, Pennsylvania; Los Angeles/Long Beach, California; Detroit, Michigan; Cleveland, Ohio; Rochester, New York; Washington, D.C. (1990 Census).

CALIFORNIA · MICHIGAN · PENNSYLVANIA · NEW YORK · ILLINOIS · OHIO · NEW JERSEY · CONNECTICUT · MASSACHUSETTS · FLORIDA

Region of origin

Italy

Some Italian immigrants also arrived in the United States via Italian communities in Argentina, Canada, and Australia.

Population

U.S.: 15,723,555 (2000 census); Canada: 1,207,475 (1996 census).

Language

Italian, Italian regional dialects (Sicilian, Neapolitan, Calabrese, Abruzzese, Genovese), English.

Dates of major arrivals

• 1880–1924: 4.5 million immigrants fled poverty in Italy.

Jobs

Business managers, grocers, lawyers, restauranteurs, salespersons, technicians, construction workers, craftsmen.

Religion

Predominantly Roman Catholicism.

Festivals

Feast of the Giglio: in honor of San Paolino, who came from the town of Nola in southern Italy (July).
Feast of Saint Rocco: protector against the plague (July).
Feast of San Gennaro: patron saint of Naples (September).
Columbus Day Parade and Festival (October).

Community organizations

The Order of the Sons of Italy in America
The National Italian American Foundation
UNICO (Unity Neighbor Integrity Charity Opportunity)
The National Organization of Italian American Women
The American Italian Historical Association

First immigrants

An Italian, Christopher Columbus, was the first European to encounter the native peoples of North America in the Caribbean in 1492. Among the early explorers of the continent were Columbus's fellow Italians John Cabot (Giovanni Caboto), Amerigo Vespucci, Giovanni da Verrazzano, Fra Marcos de Niza, and Enrico de Tonti (for whom Tontitown, Arkansas, was later named). A group of Venetian artisans immigrated to Jamestown, Virginia, in 1621, to produce glass beads for trade with native peoples. A group of Italian Protestants (Waldensians) immigrated to New York and Delaware in 1657 to escape religious persecution in Italy.

Names

Amoroso, Bono, Barbera, Cortese, D'Amico, D'Angelo, Donato, Gambino, Infante, LaPuma, Monaco, Preziosi, Provenzano, Satriani, Russo, Tagliaferro.

Food

Pasta, pizza, polenta, mozzarella, ricotta, tomato sauce (gravy, sugo), pesto sauce, Italian bread, panettone, canoli, sfogliatelle, wine, and espresso and cappuccino (coffee).

A street market in Little Italy in New York City in the 1950s. By the 1990s most Italian Americans had moved out of these urban areas to live in nearby surburban towns.

resources and manpower of their society. The majority of Italian peasants had to work as day laborers or sharecroppers (tenant farmers). The Bourbon regime had prohibited people from this poor background from emigrating; but when the new republican government ended this prohibition in 1861, migration to the United States and Canada began.

Economic conditions in Italy, especially in the more agrarian southern Italy, worsened during the 1870s and 1880s because of drought, phylloxera (a devastating plant disease), and foreign trade tariffs, or charges imposed by foreign governments on imported goods. Slowly, Italian peasants and laborers became aware of new possibilities. Many peasants and laborers, mostly from the south, who had lived their entire lives in medieval hilltop villages left for the cities of a rapidly industrializing America. In the 1870s 56,000 Italians emigrated to the United States; in the 1880s, another 307,000. Immigration peaked during the first decade of the 20th century, when over two million Italians emigrated to the United States. By the time the government passed the Immigration Act of 1924—the "National Origins Act," which limited immigration from any specific nation to a percentage of people of that nationality resident in the United States at the time of the 1890 census—a total of 4.5 million Italians had arrived on American shores.

Immigrant Labor

Of this great wave of immigrants 70 percent were men—this percentage was even higher before 1900. Nearly half of these immigrants returned to Italy at least once. Some stayed there. But most returned to North America and, in time, either brought their families over to join them or established new families in their adopted country. In the late 19th century many Italian men and boys found their way to the United States with the help of *padroni* (or *padrones*), labor agents who negotiated contracts with U.S. employers such as railroads, mine owners, construction companies, and factories. The *padroni* were both a blessing and a curse. They helped illiterate and unskilled Italian peasants secure employment in various parts of the United States and often loaned their clients money for steamship passage across the Atlantic. However, they also frequently required laborers to give them a high percentage of their wages or to repay loans for their passage at high rates of interest. In spite of the 1885 Foran Act, which outlawed

Notable Italian Americans

Tony Bennett, singer.
Enrico Caruso, opera singer.
Francis Ford Coppola, film director.
Mario Cuomo, politician.
Don DeLillo, author.
Robert De Niro, film actor.
Joe DiMaggio, baseball player.
John Fante, author.
Ella Grasso, politician.
Rudolph Giuliani, politician.
Fiorello LaGuardia, politician.
Madonna, singer.
Rocky Marciano, boxer.
Dan Marino, football player.
Dean Martin, singer.
Joe Montana, football player.
Al Pacino, film actor.
Camille Paglia, academic.
Martin Scorsese, film director.

contract labor, the *padrone* system operated through the first decade of the 20th century. After this time family and community employment networks eliminated the need for the *padroni*.

Immigrant Occupations

The immigrants had, in fact, by the early part of 20th century established themselves in a variety of occupations. Throughout the United States unskilled Italians accepted underpaid jobs in the mining, agricultural, manufacturing, construction, textile, and food-processing industries. At the same time, other workers brought their European skills and artisanship to smaller businesses such as restaurants, tailoring establishments, and stonecutters' workshops. Italian women also joined the labor force during this period. Many (35 percent) worked in the textile industry as factory seamstresses or stay-at-home piece workers—workers paid by the piece of work.

In New York Italians had their greatest influence in the construction industry, establishing a number of successful private companies and providing the bulk of the labor force for the construction of municipal projects such as the city's subway lines. In San Francisco immigrants from Genoa, Tuscany, and Sicily, who arrived via Ellis Island and the transcontinental railroad, often worked as fishermen—men such as the father of baseball legend Joe DiMaggio. In Louisiana immigrants recruited in and brought over directly from southern Italy worked mainly as sharecroppers, agricultural day laborers, and dockworkers. In Vermont they worked as stonecutters; in Chicago as meatpackers; in Pennsylvania and West Virginia as miners. Some even worked in the wilds of states like Maine and Washington, usually in lumbering camps. During the first three decades of the 20th century they made great contributions to the American economy.

In 1924 the National Origins Act and Mussolini's fascist regime in Italy slowed Italian immigration to a trickle and limited immigrants' contact with the native country. Italians in North America began a long process of economic advancement. The first generation of American-born Italians continued to work in their parents' occupations, but they also became merchants, salespeople, teachers, policemen, firemen, government officials, labor leaders, secretaries, autoworkers, restaurateurs, entertainers, and even, in limited numbers, bankers, accountants, doctors, lawyers, and artists. The Bank of America, for example, was founded in 1930 by an Italian American, Amadeo Pietro Giannini.

Throughout the 1930s, 1940s, and 1950s Italian Americans continued to accumulate wealth. They left

| Rudolph Giuliani |

In the span of a decade Rudolph Giuliani became an American icon. As a federal prosecutor during the 1980s Giuliani broke the back of Italian American organized crime. His reputation as an effective crime fighter helped win Giuliani the 1993 New York City mayoral election. Once in office, Giuliani reformed a wasteful city government and cracked down on street crime. Giuliani's methods were often labeled authoritarian and racist, but during his two terms as mayor New York City's crime rate fell to its lowest level in three decades. In the aftermath of the September 11, 2001, terrorist attacks on the United States Giuliani, in his final few months as mayor, emerged as a national symbol of strength in the face of adversity. Even after giving up political office, Giuliani remained one of the most popular figures in American politics.

Native-born American workers were frequently hostile toward Italians and other immigrants, who, they believed, posed a threat to their livelihood. On occasion, this resentment of the Italian presence erupted into violence. On March 14, 1891, following the assassination of the New Orleans Chief of Police, David Hennessy, a mob of that city's residents lynched a group of 11 Italian dockworkers who had been falsely accused and then acquitted of Hennessy's murder. (The illustration below shows the mob breaking into the prison where the Italians were being held.) Other lynchings and episodes of anti-Italian violence persisted, especially in the Midwest and South, through the 1920s.

behind the "Little Italies," where so many immigrants had lived and worked, for the single-family homes and commuter lifestyles of the American suburbs.

Stereotypes of Italian Americans

From the time they began arriving in great numbers in the 1870s and 1880s, Italians have been lumbered with both good and bad stereotypes. Some of the so-called positive stereotypes imposed on Italians is that they have closely knit families and are a religiously devout group who are diligent workers. There are also negative assumptions, for instance, in the late 19th and early 20th centuries many Americans believed that Italian immigrants were bomb-throwing anarchists. But the most long-lasting stereotype Italians have had to contend with is America's perception of them as criminals or members of the Mafia.

The Mafia is also known in America as the Cosa Nostra, which means "Our Thing." It began in Sicily as a network of underground groups committed to resisting the many foreign powers that governed the island before Italy's unification. Over the years, and especially during the 19th century, these groups developed into criminal organizations, demanding money and obedience from villagers in return for protection and influence with corrupt local officials.

In reality only a tiny percentage of Italian immigrants in North America were members of criminal organizations. However, some thinkers and the press chose to play on Americans' traditional fear of foreigners. During the years of mass immigration from Italy social theorists claimed that people from Mediterranean or southern European countries were racially inferior to northern Europeans. This was the time when nativism (the policy of favoring native inhabitants) was at its peak, and there was suspicion among extreme groups such as the Klu Klux Klan against illiterates and Catholics. American newspapers ran numerous embellished accounts of Italian involvement in crime. *The New York Times* even defended the 1891 lynching of the Italians in New Orleans on the grounds that America had to defend itself against "descendants of bandits and assassins."

During the early years of the 20th century Italian Americans were also stereotyped as political radicals bent on bringing communism and anarchy to America. It is true that many Italian immigrants, notably the newspaper editor and activist Carlo Tresca, took part in the American labor movement and were communists or anarchists—people committed to doing away with the free-market capitalist system. Public fear of such men culminated in the "red scare" in the decades following World War I (1914–1918). This fear expressed itself in the trial and 1927 execution of Nicola Sacco and Bartolomeo Vanzetti, two Italian immigrant anarchists charged with the 1920 killing of a factory security guard in South Braintree, Massachusetts.

In their trial and death Sacco and Vanzetti became international symbols of capitalist societies' political paranoia. Their plight also awakened among Italian immigrants a sense of unity and of an Italianness that transcended powerful regional differences.

During the Prohibition era (1919–1931) Al Capone, one of many criminals who supplied the Americans with illegal alcohol, added to the Mafia legend by flaunting his lavish lifestyle and mocking the federal prosecutors who eventually sent him to prison. Since Capone the image of the Mafia don—the head of a Mafia "family"—has appealed to Americans as a symbol of the nation's outlaw tradition and resistance to both government neglect and social conformity. Carlo Gambino and John Gotti—both renowned Mafia dons from New York—became models for film and television dons, and this in turn perpetuated the Italian American criminal stereotype.

By the end of the 1930s Italian Americans were generally not seen as a danger to capitalism, though they still suffered discrimination. When the United States entered World War II, Italian Americans became objects of suspicion. The government forcibly removed Japanese, German, and Italian Americans from their homes along the American coasts to internment camps for "enemy aliens" in the nation's interior. Most of the victims of this forced removal were Japanese Americans, but several hundred Italian Americans were interned for a brief time in Montana. Since World War II Italian Americans have suffered less and less from stereotyping, despite the public's continuing fascination with the Mafia and its culture.

Social Life and Politics

Like their village-dwelling predecessors, Italian immigrants of the late 19th and early 20th centuries relied almost exclusively on their families, friends, and acquaintances for support. A father was expected to provide money for his family's needs, while a mother was expected to cook, clean, look after the children, and, if she could, supplement her husband's income by working in a factory or out of her home. For their part, children were expected to attend school and, when old enough, to work and contribute money to the family.

Beyond their families immigrants relied on *paesani*—distant relations, friends, and acquaintances from the same village. In the Little Italies of this era immigrants often spoke the same regional or local dialect as their neighborhood greengrocer, butcher, and baker, just as they often knew and relied on neighborhood political bosses.

Like other immigrants, Italians relied on local, frequently corrupt, politicians, who could bring government resources to their neighborhoods in return for the immigrants' votes for their parties' candidates. Organizing their power bases around local political

| Frank Sinatra |

During the 1930s Italian Americans had a great influence on the music scene. One of the most popular entertainers of the 20th century was Frank Sinatra (1915–1998), who rose to fame in those years. Sinatra was the son of Italian immigrants and grew up in Hoboken, New Jersey. In his early days he had a following of teenage girls. Later he became a symbol of mature masculinity, with his smooth voice and sophisticated "look."

"clubs," urban Italian American politicians like James March of New York City paved the way for Italian American politicians of later years. One of them was Vito Marcantonio, a congressman from the East Harlem section of New York City. From the 1930s to the 1950s Marcantonio promoted socialist policies and won continual reelection despite the nation's increasing conservatism. After Marcantonio Italian American politics moved gradually to the right, although a majority of Italian American politicians and voters remained Democrats into the 1980s.

Italian Americans Today

Today, approximately nine million Italian Americans are part of the labor force. Of them 18 percent work in low and mid-level administrative positions; 13 percent in professional specialties; 13 percent as salespeople; 13 percent in service industries; 11 percent as laborers and factory operatives; 10 percent are executives and high-level administrators; and 10 percent are craftsmen and repairmen. About 5 percent of Italian Americans are government workers.

Individually, Italian Americans have reached the highest levels of business and the government. Lee Iacocca was president and chairman of the auto company Chrysler, and Leonard Riggio is the president of the national bookstore chain Barnes and Noble. In 1984 Congresswoman Geraldine Ferraro became the first woman candidate for vice president, while Mario Cuomo, who was then governor of New York State, nearly became the Democratic presidential candidate in 1988 and 1992.

On June 29, 1970, thousands poured into Columbus Circle in New York City to celebrate the first Italian American Unity Day and to protest negative images of Italian Americans in popular culture.

One area in which Italians have played an important role is in the arts and entertainment industry. Well-known Italian Americans in the music world include Connie Francis, Madonna, Dean Martin, and Bruce Springsteen; in the film world directors Francis Ford Coppola, Nancy Savoca, and Martin Scorsese and actors Anne Bancroft (Anna Italiano), Robert DeNiro, Al Pacino, Sylvester Stallone, John Travolta, and Leonardo di Caprio; in the literary world John Ciardi, Gregory Corso, Don DeLillo, Diane Di Prima, Mario Puzo, Richard Russo, and Gay Talese; and in the art world Joseph Stella and Frank Stella.

In recent years Italian American scholars and writers have raised the public's consciousness of Italian American contributions to all aspects of American life. Today many Italian Americans can not only identify themselves as Italian, but can also trace their roots and traditions to specific regions and villages.

See also

- Anti-immigrant prejudice (Volume 1)
- Assimilation (Volume 1)
- Crime (Volume 3)
- Family patterns (Volume 4)

Jamaicans

Jamaicans come from the English-speaking Caribbean island of Jamaica, which has a population of over 2.5 million. Traditionally, Jamaicans who have emigrated to the United States have settled on the East Coast. Today around 59 percent of Jamaican Americans—or "Jamericans," as they are known—live in cities such as New York, particularly around Brooklyn, and in Hartford, Connecticut. There are also concentrations of Jamericans in Miami and Chicago, and in Toronto in Canada, where in August each year a Caribbean celebration organized by Jamaican Americans regularly attracts over 300,000 visitors.

Jamaican Americans represent the largest group of migrants from the Caribbean. They are well established and integrated within their communities, and provide a focal point for other migrating Anglo-Caribbean groups.

Waves of Immigration

Although mass migration to the United States did not begin until 1965, there have been three major migrations of Jamaicans to the United States since the first arrivals in 1619. Even though Jamaicans traveled north earlier, along with other Caribbean migrants, they were not counted as a separate ethnic group until the 1970 census. Between 1900 and the 1920s small numbers of Caribbean migrants arrived (officially 12,245 in 1924) and continued to do so from the 1930s to the mid-1960s. During this time only 100 Jamaicans a year were allowed to enter. Since Jamaica was a British colony, most went to Great Britain.

In 1965 Great Britain changed its immigration policy with respect to its black colonies, and Jamaicans were no longer able to obtain automatic British citizenship. At the same time, the United States relaxed its immigration laws, allowing for a massive increase in Caribbean immigrants. From 1960 to 1965, 8,335 Jamaicans immigrated; from 1966 to 1970 the number jumped to 62,676. Numbers of Jamaican immigrants grew again in the 1980s—136,222 entered between 1986 and 1990—but dropped to 90,731 between 1991 and 1995. However, unofficial estimates suggest that there are at least one million Jamaicans living in the United States, many of whom are illegal immigrants. The migration of such a large segment of the population has deprived Jamaica of many of its skilled and professional workers.

Jamaican Lifestyles

Jamaican Americans' lives reflect the diversity of their culture. Many, particularly first- and second-generation immigrants, are hard workers, employed in fields such as the health sector, living in middle-income

Jamaican women playing traditional steel drums in a Labor Day street parade held by Brooklyn's large Jamaican community.

Jamaican politics

Jamaican Americans have long been politically active, starting with Marcus Garvey, who championed black emancipation in the 1920s. Jamaicans are involved in every level of politics. In New York City and Miami, for instance, they have fought discrimination to empower Jamaican and other black Americans. In 2001 Secretary of State Colin Powell became the highest-ranking American of Jamaican parentage.

17

Fact File: JAMAICANS

Distribution

- 59% live in the Northeast region, particularly in the New York metropolitan area of Brooklyn.
- 31% live in the South, especially around Miami.
- Chicago, Illinois, has another large concentration of Jamaican Americans.

Chicago

New York City

Miami

Region of origin

Jamaica

Jamaica is an island in the West Indies in the Caribbean.

Population

United States: 536,000 (2000 census)—unofficial estimates in 2001 suggest there are more than one million Jamaicans in the United States, many of them illegal immigrants.
Canada: 188,770 (1996 census).

Language

English and Jamaican *Patois*. Rastafarians speak an unofficial "Afro-Jamaican."

Community organizations

Jamaican Progressive League; Jamaican Canadian Association; Jamaican Association of Northern California.

Useful websites

Canadian Jamaican Association (www.jcassoc.com)
Embassy of Jamaica (www.emjam-usa.org)
Jamaican American Club (www.geocities.com/JamaicanAmerican Club/island.html)

Dates of major arrivals

The three major immigration waves, 1900–1920, 1930s–mid-1960s, and 1965–present, were due to better economic prospects in the U.S.

First immigrants

- 1619: 20 voluntary indentured workers arrived in Jamestown, Virginia, with the status of "free persons."

Names

Typical English surnames.

Notable Jamaican Americans

Louise Bennett-Coverly ("Miss Lou"), folklorist, poet laureate.
Marcus Garvey, early civil rights campaigner.
Colin Powell, Secretary of State.
Sheryl Lee Ralph, actress.

Religion

Various branches of Christianity, including Baptist, Methodist, and Roman Catholic. Some small groups of Hindus, Jews, Muslims, and Bahais. Rastafari is the most famous Afro-Caribbean religion, whose followers included Bob Marley.

Festivals

Independence Day, celebrated on the first Monday in August. Christian festivals. Bob Marley's Birthday in February. Labor Day, celebrated with other Caribbean groups on May 23.

Food

Ackee (fruit); saltfish (dried, salted cod); cassava (root vegetable); yams; soups, stews, gumbos (spicy meat or seafood dish served with rice), and meat or fish dishes flavored with ginger, allspice, or jerk (spicy blend for barbecuing).

white suburbs, attending church, and raising their children to value a good education. However, there has been a general misconception among the white community that many Jamaicans are welfare recipients who deal in drugs and take part in other illegal activities. While that may be true for a small minority, this stereotype does not reflect how most Jamaican Americans live.

Such is the rate of Jamaican immigration to the United States that there are Jamaicans in all 50 states. In New York City and Miami the high concentrations of Jamaican Americans have led to their neighborhoods being nicknamed "Little Jamaica" and "Kingston 22."

Jamaicans work in a variety of professions, from law, academia, and medicine to construction. A large number of Jamaicans are entrepreneurs. In cities such as New York Jamaicans have opened businesses like grocery stores selling Caribbean foods, beauty salons specializing in black hair styling, and music stores selling reggae. Many Jamaican Americans send money back to their relatives; this income is an essential part of the Jamaican economy.

Since the economy in Jamaica remains depressed, most immigrants consider their move to the United States to be long term, if not permanent. They make an effort to adapt to their new country, but this is not always easy. Normal family life can be especially hard to re-create, since more Jamaican women than men emigrate, and many leave their children behind to be raised by relatives. Even after spouses and children are reunited in the United States, the lengthy separations can result in long-term family disruption.

Arts and Culture

Music, particularly reggae, is a vital part of Jamaican life. Reggae music, popularized in North America in particular by Bob Marley and the Wailers, is the most widely known Caribbean music form. Originally from the working classes, the music was created as a means of social comment. It is closely linked with Rastafarianism, an Afro-Caribbean religion established by Haile Selassie (Ras Tafari) in 1953. Rastafarian men are easily recognizable by their dreadlock hair and colorful clothes, which are predominantly red, green, and gold. Some estimates suggest there are as many as 80,000 "Rastas" living in Brooklyn and New York City.

Dancing is an important part of Jamaican culture, and their folk dances of Jan Canoe (also known as Jonkonnu) and Accompong, originally from Africa, remain popular at Jamaican parties. As well as being cricket lovers, Jamericans are also huge soccer fans. Soccer attracts many Jamaican followers, both as spectators and as players.

Traditional Rastafarian goods are sold in this store on Liberty Street in Miami, Florida.

Cricket

Jamaicans are fanatical about cricket, an enduring legacy of British rule in the Caribbean. There are cricket leagues in New York and Washington states—with some players competing at the international level—and smaller clubs have been set up by expatriate Jamaicans, along with other Anglo-Caribbeans. Jamaicans closely follow their national cricket team, the West Indies (or "Windies").

See also

- African Americans (Volume 1)
- Barbadians (Volume 1)
- Caribbean peoples (Volume 2)
- Guyanese (Volume 4)

Useful websites

Guide to Japan
(www.japan-guide.com)
Japanese American Internment
(www.oz.net/~cyu/internment/
main.html)
Japanese American National
Museum
(www.janm.org/main.htm)
Japanese Language
(http://japanese.about.com)
Japan Information Network
(http://jin.jcic.or.jp)
Library of Congress: Japan, A
Country Study (http://memory.loc.
gov/frd/cs/jptoc.html)

In 1890, when significant numbers of Japanese immigrants began to arrive in the United States, the Japanese American population stood at 2,039. Throughout the 20th century the population has continued to grow with a significant increase following World War II (1939–1945) and continuing into the 1970s. The 2000 United States Census counted 796,700 Japanese Americans, the majority of whom lived in the West Coast states and Hawaii. While each generation of Japanese Americans has continued to assimilate, Japanese Americans also maintain their ethnic ties.

The History of Japanese American Immigration

The first Japanese immigrants consisted mostly of single men arriving from either Japan or Hawaii. Most came from rural areas and tended to cluster on the West Coast and, increasingly, in California. The percentage of the total population of Japanese Americans who lived in California rose steadily from 41.7 percent in 1900 to 73.8 percent in 1940. Another 15 percent also lived in Oregon and Washington in 1940.

The new Japanese arrivals usually found low-paid work. In British Columbia and parts of the Northwest United States large numbers of Japanese immigrants worked in lumber camps. Later, many Issei, or first-generation Japanese Americans, made quick if limited economic advances. In agriculture, which employed about one-half of Japanese Americans by 1919, many Issei used their skills, energy, and labor to achieve at least a steady prosperity. Those immigrants who became agricultural proprietors most often grew labor-intensive specialty crops, including flowers and various fruits and vegetables. Although barred from skilled occupations because labor unions would not accept them, many urban Issei similarly moved from domestic work or manual labor to establishing small businesses, working for other Japanese American businessmen, or selling Japanese American-grown produce. Most Issei did not engage in direct economic competition with white Americans.

Most Issei lived segregated lives due in part to the typical immigrant desire to live with people of a common culture. However, a hostile white majority also enforced this segregation—the Issei faced hostility from white Americans that grew out of racism and an anti-Chinese tradition on the West Coast. Japanese immigrants could not become citizens of the United States because the Naturalization Act of 1870 made them

Keeping in touch with their ethnic roots, young Japanese American dancers perform at the annual Nisei Week parade in the "Little Tokyo" area of Los Angeles, California.

Fact File: JAPANESE

Distribution

Most populous states:
- California: 288,854, or 36%
- Hawaii: 201,764, or 25%
- Washington: 35,985, or 4.5%
- Illinois: 20,379, or 2.5%

By region:
- Western states: 579,870, or 72.8%
- Southern states: 77,468, or 9.8%
- Northeast: 76,350, or 9.5%
- Midwest: 63,012, or 7.9%

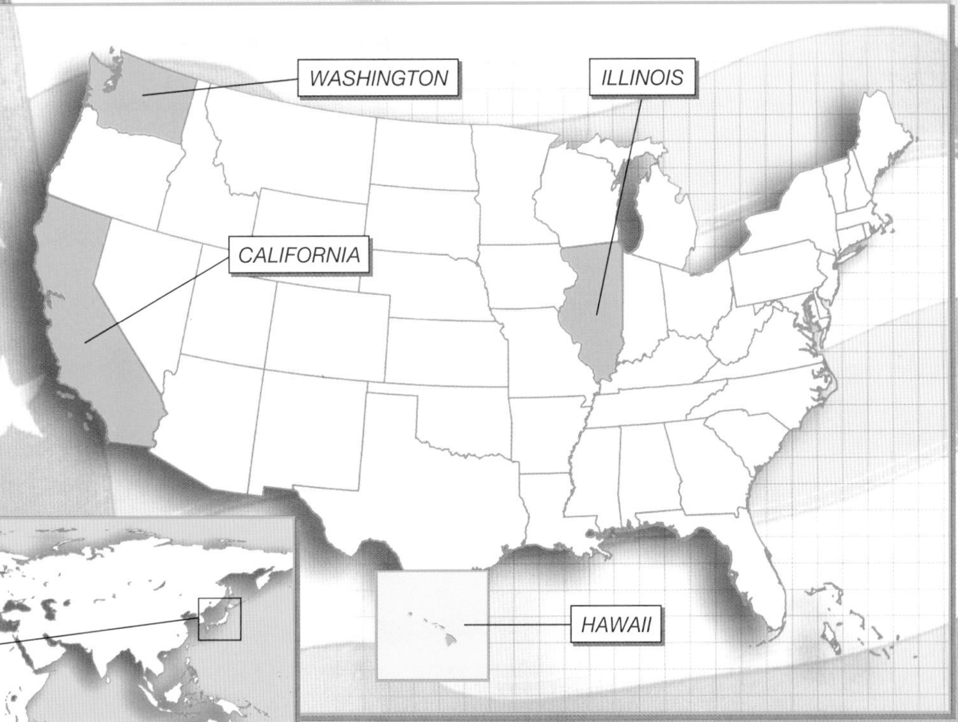

WASHINGTON

ILLINOIS

CALIFORNIA

HAWAII

Region of origin

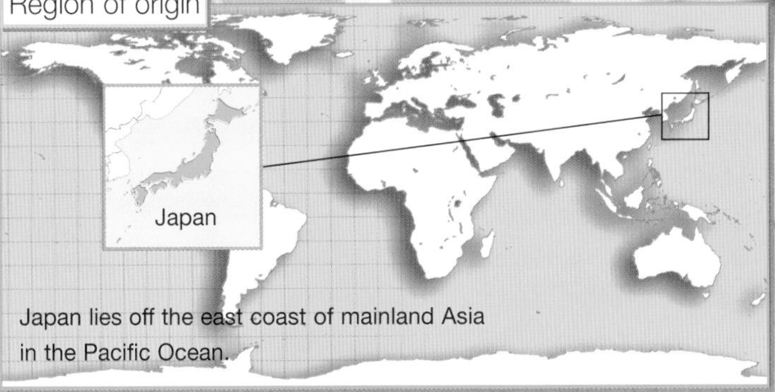

Japan

Japan lies off the east coast of mainland Asia in the Pacific Ocean.

Population

U.S.: 796,700 (2000 census);
Canada: 77,130 (1996 census).

Language

Japanese and English.

First immigrants

The earliest recorded Japanese immigrants to North America were castaways in the 1830s and 1840s, including Joseph Heco Ryûgakusei. Students emigrated as laborers to Hawaii in 1868. The short-lived Wakamatsu Colony in Gold Hill, California, was founded in 1869.

Dates of major arrivals

- Mid-19th century: individual visitors, students, merchants, and officials.
- 1890–1924: Steady immigration began in the 1890s and ended with the U.S. Immigration Act of 1924. Between 1908 and 1924 predominantly females arrived under the "Gentlemen's Agreement" of 1907–1908.

Names

Ota, Takahashi, Kobayashi, and Sakamoto.

Jobs

Mainly professional occupations such as computer engineers, healthcare workers, and lawyers.

Religion

Christianity, Buddhism, and Shintoism.

Festivals

Nisei Week: a week of celebrations in August, first held in 1934 in "Little Tokyo," Los Angeles.

Notable Japanese Americans

S. I. Hayakawa, Republican senator, California.
Spark M. Matsunaga, Democrat senator, Hawaii.
Norman Y. Mineta, Democrat, California, House of Representatives, secretary of commerce for Clinton Administration, secretary of transportation for Bush Administration.
Noriyuki "Pat" Morita, actor.
Isamu Noguchi, sculptor and designer.
Minoru Yamasaki, architect.

Community organizations

Japanese American Citizens League (www.jacl.org)
NikkeiWest, a publication for the Nisei, Sansei, and Yonsei of Northern California (www.nikkeiwest.com)
The National Japanese American Historical Society (www.nikkeiheritage.org)

Food

Various rice dishes such as *oyako-donburi* (with chicken and onion) and *unaju* (with broiled eel); soups such as *oden* (with fish cakes, bean-curd cubes, seaweed, and hard-boiled egg cooked in fish broth) and *shabu-shabu* (with sliced beef, bean curd, vermicelli, and various vegetables); *sushi* (raw fish or seafood on a ball of vinegared rice).

At the height of anti-Japanese feeling in America Japanese-owned stores such as this one suffered extensive vandalism and damage.

Notable Japanese Canadians

Joy Kogawa, author.
Ron Miki, author.
Raymond Moriyama, architect.
Kazuo Nakamura, artist.
Rick Shiomi, author.
David Suzuki, geneticist and
  environmentalist.
Shizuye Takashima, artist.
Takao Tanabe, artist .
Tamio Wakayama, artist.
Terry Watada, singer and
  songwriter.

"aliens ineligible for citizenship" by restricting citizenship only to "white persons and persons of African descent."

An anti-Japanese movement in California became significant in 1906, when the San Francisco school board's decision to place all Japanese students in segregated schools for Chinese provoked an international crisis between the United States and Japan. President Theodore Roosevelt intervened, and the school board agreed to allow Japanese students to continue to attend nonsegregated schools. In the ensuing 1907–1908 "Gentlemen's Agreement," reached between Roosevelt and Japan, the Japanese government agreed to stop issuing passports to the United States for Japanese laborers. The deal did allow, however, for the wives and children of those Japanese already residing in the United States to immigrate. Others returned to Japan to get married or arranged long-distance marriages with "picture brides." As a result, women dominated Japanese immigration after 1908.

Japanese Americans continued to face discrimination after the Gentlemen's Agreement in the form of alien land acts passed in 1913 and 1920, which denied land ownership to Japanese immigrants. They were fairly unsuccessful, however, because Issei could lease land, form landholding corporations, or put land into their children's names. The 1924 immigration act barred further Japanese immigration. Despite the racism that confronted them, many Japanese Americans had managed to achieve some degree of social mobility by the end of the 1930s. Most immigrants were at least lower middle class and could look to a future in which their children would be even better off.

World War II (1939–1945)

The Japanese military attack on Pearl Harbor on December 7, 1941, led the United States to enter World War II. Hostility toward Japanese Americans, already latent, grew to such an extent that the government decided to incarcerate all West Coast Japanese Americans in 10 isolated concentration camps. Some 120,000 Japanese Americans were imprisoned, two-thirds of whom were native-born citizens. Similar measures were taken in Canada, where Japanese Canadians were treated more harshly than their American counterparts. In mid-January 1943, however, Japanese Americans were allowed to volunteer for service in the United States military. The draft, or compulsory military conscription, was applied to Japanese Americans on January 20, 1944. This was never the case for Japanese Canadians, who were denied the opportunity of serving the armed forces throughout the war. Incarcerated Japanese Americans were gradually released from the concentration camps after going through a clearance procedure, but were not allowed to return to their homes until 1945.

Postwar Japanese American Lifestyle and Culture

Two pieces of legislation passed in the 1950s altered the status of Japanese Americans in important ways. The McCarran-Walter Immigration and Naturalization Act of 1952, passed despite the veto of President Harry S. Truman, opened immigration and naturalization to all ethnic groups. In 1959 Hawaii became the 50th state, and Hawaiian legislators provided Asian Americans with a visible presence and spokespeople in Congress.

Although Japanese Americans faced less discrimination after World War II, social barriers changed more slowly than legal ones. Segregation continued, and housing discrimination persisted into the 1960s. Japanese Americans were also labeled a "model minority" in the 1960s. This seemingly complimentary term was actually used to denigrate other immigrant groups that had not achieved the same success as Japanese Americans. Yet despite the discrimination that continued to be directed against them, Japanese Americans had, as a whole, achieved middle-class status by the 1990s.

In the 1980s Japanese Americans also struggled for and received redress for their exile and incarceration during World War II. In 1980 the Commission on Wartime Relocation and Internment of Civilians was formed by Congress to investigate government actions against Japanese Americans during World War II and to make appropriate recommendations. Its research, combined with a campaign for compensation by Japanese American community activists that had begun in the 1970s, resulted in a 1983 report that stated that exile and imprisonment had been the result of "race prejudice, war hysteria, and a failure of political leadership." The report, *Personal Justice Denied*, also recommended that the federal government formally apologize for its wartime actions and grant $20,000 to each survivor of the camps. The Civil Liberties Act of 1988 put both recommendations into effect.

Daniel Ken Inouye (1924–)

Hawaiian statehood brought a number of Japanese Americans into Congress, including Democratic Senator Daniel K. Inouye, a war hero who lost an arm while serving with the famous all-Nisei 442 Regimental Combat Team in Italy during World War II. Inouye, along with other Japanese American legislators, provided Japanese Americans with real representation in government, an important factor in promoting increasing Japanese American self-confidence after the 1950s.

Barrack-style camps, such as this relocation center in Amache, Colorado, were constructed to house the thousands of Japanese Americans incarcerated during World War II. Each family was allocated a space 20 by 25 feet (6 by 7.5 m).

Japanese American children enjoy an obento *lunch box containing several types of traditional foods at the Japanese American Community and Cultural Center in California.*

Generation names

The Japanese American community has a system of naming each generation descended from the first immigrants, who arrived toward the end of the 19th century. The first generation are known as *Issei*, while their children are known as *Nisei*. *Sansei* is the name of the third generation, *Yonsei* is the fourth generation, and the fifth generation is known as *Gosei*. Increasingly the descendants of the first generation are assimilating into mainstream American society, but new immigrants from the homeland ensure that some link with traditional Japanese culture is kept.

See also

- Anti-immigrant prejudice (Volume 1)
- Chinese (Volume 2)
- Immigrant experience (Volume 5)
- National loyalties (Volume 7)
- World War II (Volume 10)

Japanese American Generations

Generational references are less clear-cut for the groups that followed the Nisei (second-generation Japanese Americans). Indeed, the distinguishing characteristic of Japanese Americans today is their diversity. The Sansei (third generation) came of age in the 1970s along with new immigrants from Japan and a mixture of Yonsei and Gosei Japanese Americans (see box). These groups have become increasingly assimilated and feel more comfortable living with "American values." In fact, many have had few ethnic friends while growing up. They are also much less likely to have faced overt discrimination than their parents and grandparents. Yet as the Issei generation passes, so do many of the old Japanese ways.

The Sansei have gone to college in large numbers, and many enjoy gainful employment in the fields of medicine, engineering, and law. Although those Japanese Americans attending college today are quite assimilated and overwhelmingly support interracial dating and marriage, many still uphold ideals consonant with Issei and Nisei values: hard work, good education, family and community solidarity, and perseverance. Although the Sansei are more integrated than their parents, many continue to seek out and join ethnic organizations. For example, Japanese athletic leagues often draw Sansei participants who continue to stress the Japanese value of teamwork over individual effort. "Nisei Week" celebrations promoting Japanese American culture are held in Los Angeles, San Francisco, Hawaii, and elsewhere.

While the ethnic community and the Japanese family structure continue to offer Japanese Americans support, it is primarily the dominant community that offers economic opportunities. Sansei are unlikely to be found working in small ethnic businesses or farming as their grandparents did; most are instead taking advantage of higher education and increased employment opportunities to enter professional positions. The third generation is more likely to reflect the culture of its local communities than a solely ethnic culture.

Barriers to Assimilation

No matter how assimilated Japanese Americans become, they remain marked by their ethnic visibility. Stereotypes continue to limit their opportunities and present a narrow picture of Japanese Americans as a whole. While their exile and incarceration during World War II mark a watershed in Japanese American and American history, the wartime events are not the totality of the Japanese American experience. Increasingly assimilated and integrated after the war, Japanese Americans have made their own way, continuing to integrate but also maintaining associations with their ethnic community.

Jews

Although it derives from a specific religion, the identity of North American Jews has both cultural and ethnic aspects. Most American and Canadian Jews do not consider themselves to be Jewish solely on the basis of religion. While Judaism (the Jewish religion) is a binding force for the community, it is not necessary to be religious to be Jewish. In general, a person is considered to be Jewish if their mother is Jewish or if they convert to Judaism. The Jewish religion developed in the Middle East, but many people of diverse racial and ethnic origins have converted to the Jewish religion over past centuries. For example, most American Jews are of eastern European descent. Throughout history Jews were persecuted, massacred, and expelled from the European countries in which they lived. Jews have found a higher degree of acceptance in the United States than in any other country.

Jewish Population in North America

The distribution of the Jewish population in North America shifted significantly during the 20th century. While most Jews live in the large cities of the northeastern United States, movement of Jews west and south has reduced the concentration of the Jewish population in these areas. In the 1920s about 70 percent of American Jews lived in the Northeast, but by 1998 the figure had dropped to 50 percent. The number of Jews in the southern Atlantic and Pacific states, especially Florida and California, has increased significantly. By 1998 almost 40 percent of the Jewish population lived in the South or the West. By 2002 the Jewish population was dispersed throughout urban and suburban areas of the Northeast, Southeast, Midwest, and West. The main population centers in Canada are in Toronto and Montreal, with smaller communities in Vancouver and Winnipeg.

The Jewish Diaspora

The Jewish diaspora is the name given to the 2,000-year dispersion of Jews from their homeland in Palestine. It began in the first century A.D., when the Romans banned Judaism, and the Jews were forced to emigrate to the Near East, North Africa, and Europe. European Jews eventually formed two main ethnic groups: the Ashkenazim (Jews from central and eastern Europe) and the Sephardim (Jews from the Iberian Peninsula—present-day Spain and Portugal). By the 19th century four

A market in the Jewish part of New York in 1900. During the early 20th century the Jewish Lower East Side became one of the world's most crowded neighborhoods.

Fact File: JEWS

Distribution

Most populous cities:
New York (1,450,000), Los Angeles (519,000), Chicago (261,000), Boston (227,000), San Francisco (210,000), Philadelphia (206,000), Washington, D.C. (165,000), Toronto (151,000), Miami (134,000) (figures from the *American Jewish Year Book*, 1998).

Most populous states and provinces:
New York (1,652,000), California (967,000), Florida (628,000), New Jersey (465,000), Pennsylvania (282,000), Massachusetts (274,000), Illinois (269,000), Maryland (214,000), Ontario (195,000) (figures from the *American Jewish Year Book*, 1998).

NEW YORK MASSACHUSETTS ILLINOIS PENNSYLVANIA MARYLAND NEW JERSEY CALIFORNIA FLORIDA

Region of origin

Jews have immigrated to North America from virtually all parts of the globe. Some Jews lived temporarily in several different countries before settling permanently in the United States. Jewish immigrants have come from Poland, Russia, Germany, the Balkans, Lithuania, Austria-Hungary, Israel, Morocco, France, Portugal, Spain, Holland, the Middle East, and Latin America.

Jobs

The first Sephardic Jews to settle in the New World were merchants and traders. The German Jews who immigrated during the 19th century started out as peddlers but quickly became bankers, merchants, lawyers, and doctors. Later immigrants from eastern Europe also worked as peddlers or in the sweatshops of the garment industry. Jews are now highly represented in professional fields such as law, business, medicine, and the entertainment industry.

First immigrants

Jews traveled to the East Coast of North America in the early 1500s, although they did not establish any permanent settlements. In 1654, 23 Sephardic Jews traveled to New Amsterdam (now New York City) from Brazil. The first Jew known to have visited Canada was Joseph de la Penha, a Jewish trader who was driven by a storm onto the Labrador coast in the 1670s.

Names

Many Jewish first names are of Biblical origin: Aharon/Aaron, Benyamin/Benjamin, Yaacov/Jacob, Devorah/Debra, and Rivka/Rebecca. Surnames reflect the family's geographic background.

Population

United States: 5,800,000 (*American Jewish Year Book*, 1998. There are no figures from the U.S. Census Bureau, since Jewish Americans are categorized as a religious group, and the Census has not collected information on religious denomination since 1957).
Canada: 370,000 (1991 census).

Language

Hebrew is used for religious services and formal occasions. It is also the language of modern Israel. More than 30 vernacular languages were developed by the Jews of the diaspora for everyday communication. Some are nearly extinct, such as Judeo-French and Judeo-Slavic, while others such as Yiddish (a mixture of German and Hebrew) and Ladino or Judezmo (a mixture of Spanish and Hebrew) have survived.

Religion

Judaism (Conservative, Reform, Orthodox, Reconstructionist).

Festivals

Shabbat (the Sabbath) is celebrated each week. For Orthodox Jews the Sabbath falls on Saturday, while some other, less strict sects celebrate it on Sunday.
The Jewish New Year (Rosh Hashanah) falls in September or October.
Yom Kippur follows the end of Rosh Hashanah.
Holocaust Remembrance Day (April).
Israeli Independence Day (May).

million eastern European Jews lived in poverty in an area of Poland and Russia known as the Pale of Settlement, where they were subject to military conscription and heavy taxation. The Jews of western Europe received greater social and economic freedom, and some acquired wealth through banking and commerce.

Jews came to North America from many countries and cultures, resulting in economic, social, and religious differences. Immigration of Jews to North America occurred in five main waves: Sephardic Jews from the Iberian Peninsula (from the 17th to the 19th centuries), German Jews (19th century), eastern European Jews (turn of the 19th and 20th centuries), Jews fleeing Nazi Germany (1930s and 1940s), and Soviet Jews from Russia (1980s).

Sephardic Jews

In 1492 nearly 150,000 Jews were expelled from Spain and Portugal. The Sephardic Jews who later settled in North America were part of this Iberian Jewish diaspora. In 1654, 23 Sephardic Jews arrived in New Amsterdam (later known as New York). While they initially met resistance, they were eventually able to settle in the New World. They were followed by other immigrants, and by 1820 there were at least 2,500 Jews in America. The Sephardic Jews immigrated to America seeking religious tolerance and economic prosperity. Primarily shopkeepers and traders, they settled in cities along the eastern seaboard—New York, Newport, Savannah, Philadelphia, and Charleston became the largest population centers.

A poster written in English and in Hebrew from the late 19th century advertising English lessons for Jewish immigrants. Many Jewish immigrants during this period came from eastern Europe and spoke no English.

German Jews

The next wave of Jewish immigrants came during the mid-19th century, from Germany and Poland, to escape social unrest and to seek better economic opportunities. The German Jews who arrived between 1820 and 1880 did not concentrate in a few communities as the Sephardic Jews had done, but instead led the westward expansion of the Jewish population across the continent. Working as tradesmen, some settled among German farmers in Pennsylvania and others in the Midwest. Jewish peddlers, or street salesmen, followed the growth

Waves of immigration

1654–1820: more than 2,500
   Sephardic Jews
1820–1880: about 200,000
   German Jews
1880–1924: more than 2,500,000
   Jewish immigrants from eastern
   Europe
1924–1945: 250,000 middle-class
   Jewish immigrants from western
   Europe
1945–present: about 350,000 Jews
   from the former Soviet Union

of the cotton industry in the South and the gold rush in the West. With their savings they eventually opened small stores in the towns where they traded. Some of these small businesses eventually grew into famous department store chains, such as Macy's, Neiman-Marcus, and Bloomingdale's.

The Jewish population of the United States increased from 50,000 in 1850 to 230,000 in 1880. While German Jews today form a small proportion of the American Jewish population, their importance is derived from their notable financial success. They became influential businessmen and bankers at a time when American industry was developing. They were well-educated, spoke German rather than Yiddish, and embraced Reform Judaism (see box on page 30).

Eastern European Jews

The largest wave of Jewish immigrants was the eastern European Jews who arrived between 1880 and 1924. Almost one-third of the Jewish population of eastern Europe emigrated during this period because of considerable anti-Jewish violence and oppression. About 90 percent of these immigrants, or 2.5 million eastern European Jews, settled in North America. Most of the new arrivals were young, with 80 percent being between ages 15 and 45.

Relations between German Jews and eastern European Jews were often difficult because of religious and social differences. Eastern European Jews tended to cluster in distinct urban neighborhoods in the northeastern United States. They practiced Orthodox Judaism (see box on page 30) and wore skull caps, beards, and old-fashioned clothing. They were mainly poor and had little education. Their distinct appearance often made them a target for anti-Jewish behavior.

Eastern European Jews were very traditional and embraced the Yiddish (a mixture of German and Hebrew) language and culture. Language differences and the requirements of a kosher diet—food fit for consumption according to Jewish law (see box on page 29)—encouraged immigrants to stay in Jewish neighborhoods in the large cities of the East and the Midwest. More than half of eastern European Jews were manual laborers or peddlers, butchers, bakers, and grocers. Many worked in exploitative conditions in the sweatshops of the garment industry, the majority of which were owned by German Jews. Many

A Jewish rally in New York in 1933 staged as a protest against the persecution of German Jews by the Nazi government. The rally was part of a nationwide movement.

A Jewish scribe in New York working to repair the writings on a Torah scroll (the first five books of the Bible). Traditionally Torahs are handwritten and must be maintained according to Jewish law.

eastern European Jews lived on the crowded Lower East Side of Manhattan in New York City. In 1908 more than a third of households slept five or more to a room.

Immigration peaked during the year 1906, when 153,000 Jews arrived in the United States. The migration of large numbers of eastern European Jews continued until restrictive immigration laws were passed in the United States in 1924. The Immigration Restriction Act decreased annual Jewish migration to about 10 percent of previous numbers. Similar laws were passed in Canada in 1931.

Refugees from Nazi Germany

Between 1935 and 1941, 150,000 Jews were allowed to immigrate to North America. They were mainly businessmen and professionals who came as refugees from Nazi Germany. During the 1930s the Nazis set out to destroy the entire Jewish population living in Europe. Over 60 percent of the nine million Jews who lived in Europe at the beginning of World War II (1939–1945) had been massacred or sent to death camps by 1945. Despite the threat to the survival of Jewish individuals, both the United States and Canada maintained extremely strict immigration policies for Jews during this period.

Jewish immigration to North America resumed slowly after the end of World War II. Between 1945 and 1959 approximately 192,000 Jews, most from displaced-persons camps, arrived. During the 1970s Jewish immigrants began to arrive from the Soviet Union, as political and economic changes led hundreds of thousands of Soviet Jews to come to North America. These immigrants took up residence primarily in New York City or other large cities such as Los Angeles.

Foods

There is no specific cuisine associated with Judaism because of the diverse ethnic origins of Jews. For example, Sephardic Jews have a cooking style that reflects the cuisine of the Iberian Peninsula. However, under the *kashrut*, or kosher dietary rules, certain types of food are permitted or prohibited for Orthodox Jews. For example, meat from sheep and cattle is allowed, while pork is forbidden. Animals must be killed humanely, and all blood must be completely drained. Meat and dairy products cannot be cooked or eaten together.

A rabbi delivering the New Year sermon to Jewish worshipers at a congregational church. The Jewish New Year, or Rosh Hashanah, takes place in September or October.

Types of Judaism

There is a wide spectrum of religious practice within Judaism. Orthodox Judaism, which is now practiced by a minority of U.S. Jews (about 6 percent), is the most traditional form of Judaism. It pays particular attention to religious obligations, such as Jewish holidays. Conservative Judaism, the largest branch in the United States (40 percent), favors a mix of tradition with openness to change. Reform Judaism (36 percent) is the most liberal form. It was the first sect to ordain women rabbis and accept intermarriage and converts.

Jews in Canada

The majority of Jewish Canadians are of eastern European descent. While Jewish immigration from eastern Europe to the United States peaked between 1880 and 1900, immigration to Canada was concentrated between 1900 and 1920. About 126,000 Jews lived in Canada in 1925. Jewish immigration to Canada was curtailed in 1931, when Canadian immigration policy became more restrictive in response to a period of economic depression. Immigration resumed after the end of World War II, with about 34,000 Jews arriving between 1947 and 1952. Since the late 1950s about 20,000 French-speaking Jews have arrived from North Africa. During the 1980s and 1990s another 20,000 Jews migrated to Canada from the former Soviet Union.

Education and Wealth

During the 19th century most Jewish Americans worked in sweatshops and as peddlers. However, by 1890 over two-thirds of Jews of western European descent worked as retailers, bankers, brokers, wholesalers, accountants, bookkeepers, and clerks. This upward social movement of Jews in North America was unprecedented and unparalleled. In 1990, 80 percent of employed Jewish males worked at white-collar jobs, compared to 48 percent of the white male population in general. The average income of Jewish American families is the highest among all ethnic groups—72 percent above the national average.

Jews have also acquired higher levels of education. In 1990 the percentage of American Jews with a college education was double that of other white Americans. Business, law, dentistry, and medicine have been the most popular subjects to study. Today Jews hold prominent positions in government, business, journalism, science, and academia. Many of the United States' greatest scientists have been Jewish, including the physicist Albert Einstein. More than 25 percent of all Nobel prizes won by Americans were awarded to Jews.

Family Life

Jews in North America have always emphasized family life. Concepts such as *nakhus* (parental pride), *yikhus* (honorable accomplishments of the family line), peace in the household, and *besherte* (finding one's life mate) remain central to Jewish families. Despite the geographical dispersion of families, declining birthrates, increasing intermarriage, and assimilation into U.S. society, family life continues to be important for Jewish Americans. The bond between parents and children is a particularly important aspect of family life. Parents are expected to provide the basis for their children's success in return for feelings of

pride in their offspring. Children are expected to take on increasing amounts of family responsibility as part of the process of becoming a *mensch*, or a responsible or caring adult.

Arts, Media, and Culture

Jews have made a major contribution to American culture. In the 1920s the entertainment industry was dominated by Jewish composers—George and Ira Gershwin, Irving Berlin—and Jewish entertainers—the Marx Brothers, Al Jolson. By the 1930s all the major film production companies, including Warner Brothers and Twentieth Century Fox, were owned by Jews. Jewish Americans working in films today include the directors Woody Allen and Steven Spielberg.

Jewish Americans have also contributed to publishing, writing, and journalism. Many of America's best-known writers, such as Saul Bellow, J.D. Salinger, Joseph Heller, Philip Roth, and Arthur Miller, are Jewish. In addition, the renowned publishers Alfred A. Knopf, Random House, and Simon and Schuster were founded by Jews.

Political Concerns

Among the primary political concerns of North American Jews is the security of Israel, especially since 1987, when the Palestinian uprising, or Intifadah, began in the region. Israel was established in 1948 in the Near East in what was then known as Palestine. Although half of all Jews live in North America, some believe that Israel is their spiritual home. About a third of the world's Jewish population, or 4.2 million Jews, live in Israel. The United States continues to be the main supporter of Israel, and since the late 1930s American Jews have given billions of dollars in aid to Israel.

A group of Jewish Americans reciting blessings before eating food and drinking wine. There are many different blessings for different types of food and drink.

Notable Jewish Americans

Woody Allen, movie director.
Isaac Asimov, chemist, science fiction writer.
Saul Bellow, novelist.
Irving Berlin, composer.
Noam Chomsky, linguist.
Kirk Douglas, actor.
Bob Dylan, songwriter.
Albert Einstein, physicist.
George Gershwin, composer.
Allen Ginsberg, poet.
Samuel Goldwyn, film producer.
Shawn Green, baseball player.
Edward Koch, former mayor of New York City.
The Marx Brothers, comedians.
Arthur Miller, playwright.
Itzhak Perlman, violinist.
Joseph Pulitzer, journalist.
Philip Roth, novelist.
Jerry Seinfeld, comedian.
Stephen Sondheim, composer and lyricist.
Susan Sontag, essayist and novelist.
Steven Spielberg, movie director.
Mark Spitz, swimmer.
Barbra Streisand, singer.
Barbara Walters, journalist.

See also

- Germans (Volume 4)
- Israelis (Volume 6)
- Palestinians (Volume 8)
- Poles (Volume 8)
- Religion (Volume 9)
- Russians (Volume 9)

Jordanians

Jordanian festivals

Jordanian Independence Day (May 25).
In addition, Muslim Jordanians observe Islamic festivals such as Eid al-Fitr (the feast ending the month of fasting for Ramadan) and Eid al-Adah (the Feast of the Sacrifice). Christian Jordanians celebrate holidays such as Christmas and Easter.

See also

• Arab Americans (Volume 1)
• Iraqis (Volume 5)
• Israelis (Volume 6)
• Palestinians (Volume 8)
• Syrians (Volume 10)

Situated in the heart of the Middle East, Jordan serves as a crossroads between East and West. It now shares borders with Syria, Iraq, Israel, and Saudi Arabia. While Jordan has played a crucial role in striving for peace in the Middle East, tensions with Israel continue to be the most critical problem for the country.

Most Jordanians consider themselves part of the Arab world and adhere to Islamic traditions. Numerically, they form a relatively small component of the Arab American group. The first significant numbers of Jordanians left for North America after World War II (1939–1945). Most of this first wave were Orthodox Christians, but conflicts with Israel in the 1960s encouraged higher numbers of Muslims to leave. The abolition of the United States Immigration Act in the 1960s led to an overall increase in Arab immigration, with almost 7,000 arriving from 1966 to 1975; another 64,000 arrived from 1980 to 1998.

Jordanian Americans tend to be well educated and urbanized, choosing to live in large cities such as Los Angeles, Boston, and New York. Families are tightly knit and based on principles of respect for elders and mutual support of family members. Great emphasis is placed on education; the community includes a relatively high percentage of college graduates. A link to Arabic culture is provided by Arabic newspapers, radio, and television in North America.

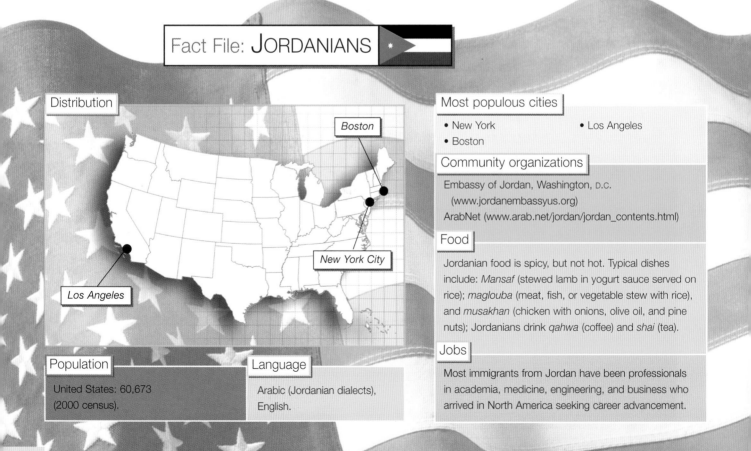

Fact File: JORDANIANS

Distribution

Boston

New York City

Los Angeles

Most populous cities

• New York
• Los Angeles
• Boston

Community organizations

Embassy of Jordan, Washington, D.C.
(www.jordanembassyus.org)
ArabNet (www.arab.net/jordan/jordan_contents.html)

Food

Jordanian food is spicy, but not hot. Typical dishes include: *Mansaf* (stewed lamb in yogurt sauce served on rice); *maglouba* (meat, fish, or vegetable stew with rice), and *musakhan* (chicken with onions, olive oil, and pine nuts); Jordanians drink *qahwa* (coffee) and *shai* (tea).

Population

United States: 60,673 (2000 census).

Language

Arabic (Jordanian dialects), English.

Jobs

Most immigrants from Jordan have been professionals in academia, medicine, engineering, and business who arrived in North America seeking career advancement.

Koreans

Koreans have been immigrating to the United States and Canada for nearly 100 years. However, the vast majority of them arrived after the passage of the 1965 Immigration Act, when the government introduced a new immigration system based mainly on reunifying families and finding people with needed skills. Today, there are over one million Korean Americans, with the largest number living in California. However, Koreans are more geographically evenly distributed than most other Asian groups, with large populations living in other large cities such as New York, Chicago, Seattle, Washington, D.C., and the San Francisco Bay area. Substantial numbers of Koreans also migrated to Canada after World War II (1939–1945) and at the end of the Korean War in 1953. While early immigrants were largely single men recruited to work on the Hawaiian sugar plantations, Korean Americans today are a diverse and heterogeneous group.

Although Koreans call their country the "Land of the Morning Calm," much of Korean immigration was caused by uncertainties in Korea throughout the 20th century. During the early part of the century Koreans came to North America to escape religious persecution and oppression by Japan. Japan took over Korea in 1876 and formally annexed it in 1910. After the Korean War the nation was firmly divided into communist North Korea and democratic South Korea, leading to the threat of potential future instability and conflict. In recent years, as the economic conditions in South Korea have improved and the threat of war with North Korea has lessened, South Korean immigration to North America has started to level off: Emigration out of North Korea is severely restricted.

Leaving the Morning Calm

The first Koreans to arrive in the United States were three political refugees who escaped after a failed attempt to overthrow the Korean monarchy in 1885. Korean immigration did not begin in earnest until January 13, 1903, when the the ship the SS *Gaelic* arrived in Honolulu, Hawaii, with 56 men, 21 women, and 25 children. From 1903 to 1905, 6,048 men, 637 women, and 541 children entered Hawaii.

Unlike many other immigrant groups who came to the United States as sojourners—people hoping to make money and return to their native countries—Koreans arrived with the

The Korean War (1950–1953) caused widespread destruction throughout Korea. As a result, many Koreans migrated to the United States and Canada.

Fact File: KOREANS

Distribution

Most populous states (2000 census):
- California: 345,882
- New York: 119,846
- New Jersey: 65,349
- Illinois: 51,453
- Texas: 45,571

Most populous cities (1990 census):
- Greater Los Angeles: 194,437
- Greater New York City: 118,096
- San Francisco Bay Area : 42,277
- Greater Washington, D.C.: 39,850

SAN FRANCISCO · ILLINOIS · NEW JERSEY · NEW YORK · CALIFORNIA · Los Angeles · New York City · Washington, D.C. · TEXAS

Region of origin

Korea

Korea is a small, mountainous country in East Asia bordered by China and Russia. Today the country is divided between North and South Korea along the 38th Parallel.

Dates of major arrivals

- 1903–1905: Approximately 7,500 Koreans came to Hawaii.
- 1953–1965: Following the Korean War (1950–1953), an estimated 10,000 Koreans immigrated to the United States, including a large number of Korean War orphans and Korean wives of U.S. servicemen.
- 1965–present: It is estimated that over 800,000 Koreans have immigrated to the United States since 1965.

Jobs

Many first-generation Korean Americans operate small businesses such as clothing and accessory stores, greengrocers, liquor stores, and dry cleaners. Second-generation Korean Americans are more likely to be found in professions such as law, medicine, or education.

First immigrants

The earliest immigrants were 7,226 men, women, and children who were brought to Hawaii on the SS *Gaelic* from 1903 to 1905. These Koreans were recruited by Hawaiian sugar plantation owners to work in the sugar cane fields.

Names

The most common Korean surname is Kim. It is estimated that 20 to 25 percent of Koreans share that name. Other common family names include Ahn, Cho, Choi, Chung, Kang, Lee, Lim, Park, Wang, and Yu.

Population

U.S.: 1,076,872 (2000 census); Canada: 66,655 (1996 census).

Language

Many theories have been proposed about the origin of the Korean language. The most likely explanation links Korean to the Altaic languages of Central Asia. Officially, there are two standard dialects, the Seoul dialect spoken in South Korea and the Pyong'yang dialect that is spoken in North Korea. Most Korean Americans speak the Seoul dialect, and 80 percent report speaking Korean with their families.

Religion

While Christians make up roughly half of the population in Korea, they account for over 90 percent of Korean Americans. Most Korean Americans are Presbyterian (42 percent), followed by Roman Catholic (14 percent) and Methodist (14 percent).

Festivals

Seol-nal (New Year) is celebrated on January 1 (Solar Calendar). Samil (Independence Day) is celebrated on March 1. This day marks the beginning of the Korean independence movement against the Japanese during their colonial rule (March 1, 1919). Ch'usok (Harvest Moon Festival, the Korean Thanksgiving).

Food

Traditional food includes *kimchee* (pickled cabbage), *bulgogi* (marinated beef), *kalbi* (beef ribs), and various *chigaes* (stews). During holidays Koreans enjoy various types of *duk* (rice cakes).

intention of making a permanent place for themselves in North America. Two reasons contributed to the Korean immigrants' desire to make North America their permanent home. First, the early immigrants were Christian converts who left Korea due to religious persecution. Second, the immigrants wanted to escape Japanese oppression in Korea. By 1905 all emigration of Koreans had been stopped by the ruling Japanese government, which was concerned with the growing anti-Japanese activities of the emigrants.

However, one group of immigrants who continued to arrive in the United States were the "picture brides," so called because men chose a bride from a photograph without meeting the women who were to become their wives. Following the 1907 Gentlemen's Agreement between the United States and Japan, Korean immigrant men were also allowed to arrange for the immigration of their wives-to-be. By 1924, when the American government stopped all Asian immigration to the United States, nearly 2,000 picture brides had arrived in America. Consequently, virtually all of the population growth between 1905 and 1965 of Korean Americans was the result of American-born Koreans.

Following the end of World War II in 1945, when Korea gained independence from Japan, Korean immigration to America began again and increased sharply during the 1950s due to the Korean War. Between 1950 and 1965 most of the Korean immigrants who came to America were the wives of American servicemen or Korean War orphans who were adopted by American citizens. It is estimated that 150,000 Korean children have been adopted by U.S. citizens since the beginning of the Korean War in 1950.

After the introduction of the 1965 U.S. Immigration Act most subsequent Korean immigrants arrived from South Korea. By 1970 the Korean population in the United States had doubled from 25,000 in 1965 to 50,000, and by 1980 that number increased over sixfold to 357,393. The Korean population doubled again by 1990 to 798,849. It is estimated that there are 1,076,872 Korean Americans living in the United States today. In Canada there is a much smaller Korean population—66,655 according to the 1996 Canadian Census. The vast majority of Korean Canadians live in Toronto. Many have become successful professionals, particularly in journalism and music.

A Promising Future

Today many first-generation Korean immigrants operate small "mom-and-pop" stores. Koreans are more likely to be small business owners than any other ethnic group, with one in four Korean Americans operating a small business. The common misconception is that most Korean Americans own small grocery stores and dry-cleaning businesses, but the most typical types of business owned by Korean Americans are clothing and accessory stores. However, few

A sign in Koreatown in Los Angeles. Koreatown was one of the areas worst affected by the 1992 L.A. riots, incurring $400 million in damage.

Notable Korean Americans

Margaret Cho, actress, comedienne, and author. She starred in *All American Girl*, the first sitcom to feature an Asian American family.

Chang-rae Lee, award-winning author of *Native Speaker* and *A Gesture Life*.

Sammy Lee, first Asian to win an Olympic gold medal for the United States (diving).

Angela E. Oh, noted attorney and civil rights activist.

See also

• Chinese (Volume 2)
• Cold War (Volume 2)
• Festivals (Volume 4)
• Japanese (Volume 6)
• National loyalties (Volume 7)
• World War II (Volume 10)

second-generation Korean Americans have opted to follow in their parents' footsteps. Instead, many second-generation Korean Americans have entered professional fields such as medicine, law, and accounting. The success of these small businesses and the movement of second-generation Korean Americans have allowed most Korean Americans to become wealthier than earlier Korean immigrants.

Maintaining Cultural Traditions

For most Korean Americans the church is the center of their social and cultural life. There are approximately 4,500 Korean churches in the United States, and nearly 80 percent of Korean Americans attend church. Unlike other East Asian immigrants, Koreans did not form clan- or region-based associations. Instead, Koreans relied on the church for making friends, forming support networks, and receiving social services. Other types of organizations that are common among Korean Americans are high school and college alumni associations, and kye groups—rotating credit associations, which are an important source of start-up capital for businesses, home improvements, or other expenses. Most Korean Americans still celebrate many traditional holidays and festivals. Ch'usok, the Korean harvest festival, is celebrated on the 14th, 15th, and 16th days of the eighth month of the lunar calendar and is a major holiday for Korean Americans.

Building a Political Base

Since the beginning of their arrival in the United States Korean Americans have been actively involved with the fate of their homeland. Early immigrants worked vigorously for the Korean independence movement from Japan, trying to bring international attention to the plight of the Korean people. Since the end of the Korean War in 1953 Korean Americans have been involved in the reunification movement to join North and South Korea.

In addition, Korean Americans became active in American politics after the Los Angeles riots in 1992 in part to improve relations with their Afro-American neighbors. During the riots much of Koreatown in the city was destroyed, resulting in $400 million in damage. After the riots many Korean American leaders began to see the need to assert their political positions. The event also had the effect of shifting the leadership of the Korean American community from first-generation small business-owners to second-generation professionals who were more skilled in political negotiation. On May 2, 1992, more than 30,000 Korean Americans marched through Koreatown in Los Angeles calling for justice for Rodney King and reparations for victims of the rioting—the largest protest ever held by Asian Americans.

Kurds

The Kurds are nomads who have lived for thousands of years in and near the Zagros Mountains in western Iran. Following the collapse of the Ottoman Empire after World War I (1914–1918), this area was divided into present-day Turkey, Iraq, Iran, Syria, and Russia. Today's "Kurdish problem" arose because the Kurds wished to form the nation promised them in the 1920 Treaty of Sèvres, but which still does not exist. In Iraq, where Kurds make up 23 percent of the population, uprisings and offensives led to a failed Kurdish revolution in 1974. Saddam Hussein's recent Iraqi regime treated the Kurds brutally, and their plight in Iraq received world attention after the Gulf War (1990–1991). Turkey also outlawed any expression of Kurdish culture despite its Kurdish population of about 12 million, and thousands have died and had their villages destroyed in ongoing unrest.

Many of the Iranian, Iraqi, and Turkish refugees who emigrate to Canada and settle in Toronto and southern Ontario are of Kurdish heritage. In the United States some have formed large Iraqi communities, such as that in Detroit, Michigan, and there are many small Kurdish communities in California. Many Kurdish North Americans continue to campaign for public awareness of the plight of Kurds in the Middle East, but this has been complicated recently by the U.S.-directed War against Terrorism.

Newroz

On March 21 the Kurdish holiday Newroz, or "new day" in Kurdish, celebrates both the arrival of spring and the beginning of the Kurdish New Year. According to Kurdish legend, Newroz marks the day that a Kurdish ironsmith named Kawa killed the cruel Assyrian King Dehak and liberated the Kurds and other peoples in the Middle East. Kawa lit a large fire on a mountaintop to signal a new era and to proclaim freedom throughout the land.

See also

- Iranians (Volume 5)
- Iraqis (Volume 5)
- Syrians (Volume 10)
- Turks (Volume 10)

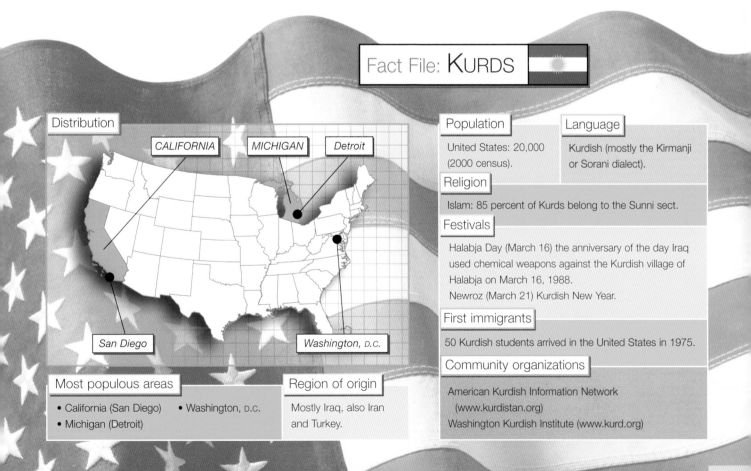

Fact File: KURDS

Distribution

CALIFORNIA   MICHIGAN   Detroit

San Diego   Washington, D.C.

Most populous areas

- California (San Diego)
- Michigan (Detroit)
- Washington, D.C.

Region of origin

Mostly Iraq, also Iran and Turkey.

Population

United States: 20,000 (2000 census).

Language

Kurdish (mostly the Kirmanji or Sorani dialect).

Religion

Islam: 85 percent of Kurds belong to the Sunni sect.

Festivals

Halabja Day (March 16) the anniversary of the day Iraq used chemical weapons against the Kurdish village of Halabja on March 16, 1988.
Newroz (March 21) Kurdish New Year.

First immigrants

50 Kurdish students arrived in the United States in 1975.

Community organizations

American Kurdish Information Network (www.kurdistan.org)
Washington Kurdish Institute (www.kurd.org)

Kuwaitis

Community organizations

Embassy of Kuwait, Ottawa,
   Canada (www.embassyof
   kuwait.com)
Kuwait Cultural Office
   (www.kuwaitculture.com)
Kuwait Information Office
   (www.kuwait-info.org)
National Union of Kuwaiti Students
   (www.nuks.org)—in Arabic

See also

• Arab Americans (Volume 1)
• Iraqis (Volume 6)

Kuwait is a small country in the Middle East, located on the Persian Gulf and bordered by Iraq and Saudi Arabia. It is slightly smaller than New Jersey and consists largely of flat desert. Since World War II (1939–1945) Kuwait has enjoyed high standards of living, healthcare, and education created by wealth derived from its vast oil fields. The country became independent in 1961. Kuwaitis are predominantly Sunni Muslims, although there is a large Shi'ite Muslim minority. The official language is Arabic, but Kuwaiti schoolchildren are taught English from the age of 10.

Specific data are not available for Kuwaiti immigrants to the United States because the Census Bureau classifies them in a general Arab category. However, the small Kuwaiti population means that the numbers of immigrants to North America have been fairly low. During the late 19th and early 20th centuries Kuwaitis began to join other Arab immigrants in North America. These early arrivals came seeking new financial opportunities. Immigrants today tend to be students, professionals, and businessmen. After the Iraqi invasion of Kuwait in 1990 hundreds of thousands fled, and a significant number were offered Temporary Protected Status in the United States until conditions at home improved. They began to return after the reestablishment of Kuwaiti sovereignty in 1991.

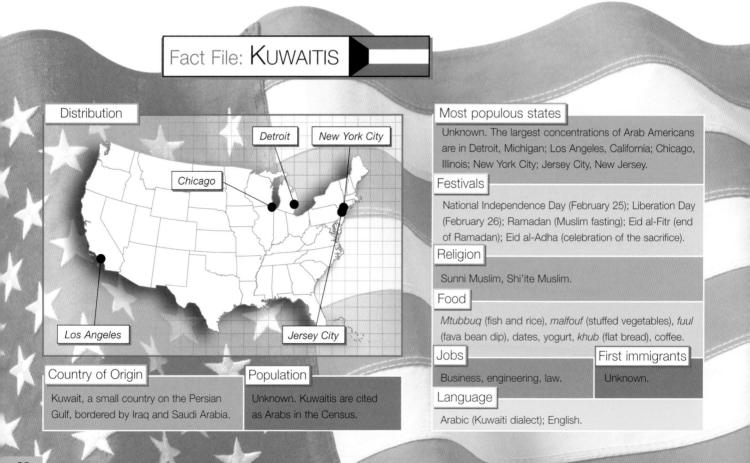

Fact File: KUWAITIS

Distribution

Detroit · New York City · Chicago · Los Angeles · Jersey City

Most populous states

Unknown. The largest concentrations of Arab Americans are in Detroit, Michigan; Los Angeles, California; Chicago, Illinois; New York City; Jersey City, New Jersey.

Festivals

National Independence Day (February 25); Liberation Day (February 26); Ramadan (Muslim fasting); Eid al-Fitr (end of Ramadan); Eid al-Adha (celebration of the sacrifice).

Religion

Sunni Muslim, Shi'ite Muslim.

Food

Mtubbuq (fish and rice), *malfouf* (stuffed vegetables), *fuul* (fava bean dip), dates, yogurt, *khub* (flat bread), coffee.

Jobs

Business, engineering, law.

First immigrants

Unknown.

Language

Arabic (Kuwaiti dialect); English.

Country of Origin

Kuwait, a small country on the Persian Gulf, bordered by Iraq and Saudi Arabia.

Population

Unknown. Kuwaitis are cited as Arabs in the Census.

Labor unions

A labor union is an organization made up of employees, and in the United States and Canada many unions have a long tradition of high numbers of ethnic members and association with ethnic groups. The purpose of a union is to bargain with an employer over working conditions, pay, and other issues that affect workers. Labor unions have four main activities: They recruit new members, they negotiate with employers on behalf of their members, they organize strikes when necessary, and they become politically involved by lobbying for their interests or supporting politicians who favor labor unions.

In the 18th century in North America there were very few labor laws, and workers tended to move from employer to employer. From 1860 to 1900 the United States became the world's greatest industrialized nation, and in the 1860s the first national unions were formed. The first labor unions, such as the AFL (American Federation of Labor), represented mainly white, skilled craftsmen and were reluctant to admit unskilled workers and ethnic minorities.

Immigrants and Labor Unions

Immigrants began to play a part in U.S. labor unions in the mid-1800s when many of them started working in manufacturing industries. In New England, for example, mill owners started to recruit immigrants, usually Irish, as well as others from England, France, Germany, and Canada, to work in their factories. These immigrants often replaced young, local girls who left the factories in order to get married and to escape the very harsh working conditions.

As more and more immigrants began arriving, those who left their jobs because of poor working conditions were easily replaced. In 1846, for instance, when a group of Irish workers in New York City went on

Useful websites

American Federation of Labor and Congress of Industrial Organizations (www.aflcio.org)
Croatian Workers' Benefit Society (www.croatianfraternalunion.org)
Industrial Workers of the World (www.iww.org)
International Brotherhood of Teamsters (www.teamsters.org)

Jimmy Hoffa

James R. Hoffa (1913–1975) was the president of the International Brotherhood of Teamsters from 1957 to 1971. A controversial labor leader, he was known for his tough bargaining and his connections with organized crime. During the 1950s and 1960s he helped build the Teamsters into the largest union organization in the United States. In 1967 he was sentenced to 13 years in prison for stealing union pension funds. Released from prison early, in 1971, he tried to regain his position as president. However, in 1975 he disappeared in Detroit. It is widely believed that he was killed by the local mafia.

Members of the Industrial Workers of the World, or IWW, demonstrating in New York in 1914. They were against sending workers to fight in World War I.

Many immigrants, such as these Chinese textile workers in a 1930s sweatshop in San Francisco, were not represented by labor unions.

Samuel Gompers

Samuel Gompers was born in 1850 in London, England, to Dutch-Jewish parents. He came to the United States in 1863, already an apprenticed cigarmaker. Gompers wanted to support workers like himself. In 1886 he founded the American Federation of Labor, serving as its president for 37 years. His emphasis on "bread and butter" unionism, rejecting political activism, helped shape organized labor in the United States.

See also

• Immigrant experience (Volume 5)
• Native American workers (Volume 8)
• Trades and professions (Volume 10)

strike to raise wages from 65 cents a day to 87½ cents a day, the employer broke the strike by hiring German immigrants.

As a result, some immigrant groups banded together to form their own labor groups, including the Croatian Workers' Benefit Society. The organization was set up to protect Croatians who worked in Pittsburgh's low-paying, high-risk steel industry. By the mid-1800s some immigrant groups dominated certain professions. For example, Italians worked in the construction industry, Jews in the garment industry, and Irish immigrants in transportation. It is not uncommon to find local labor unions consisting almost entirely of one ethnic group.

Twentieth-Century Labor Unions

In the 1930s there was a move among unions to recruit millions of unskilled workers, many of whom were immigrants. For many immigrants the labor movement was a means to become Americanized. The unions not only protected jobs, but in some cases provided legal assistance for those workers who sought U.S. citizenship.

Despite the increase in the numbers joining unions, certain immigrant groups still faced exclusion and were forced to set up their own organizations. The Brotherhood of Sleeping Car Porters was officially recognized in 1937 and became the first successful black-led trade union in the United States. It was founded by black porters who worked on the railroads. They wanted to improve their working conditions—they worked 400 hours per month for less than $100.

Another immigrant group that had to fight hard were Mexican Americans. In the 1920s Mexican farm laborers working in the Southwest were not allowed to join the AFL because the union claimed that they were "unskilled" workers. So, the Mexicans started their own unions for railroad workers and for fruit pickers. In the 1930s Mexicans became more active in union work, and the Cannery and Agricultural Workers Industrial Union organized a strike of 12,000 cotton pickers in 1933. In the 1960s activist César Chávez founded the National Farm Workers Association to protect migrant Mexican farmworkers.

Today, the main labor organization in the United States is the American Federation of Labor and Congress of Industrial Organizations (AFL/CIO). It is an association of national unions and is financed by payments from its members. Its Canadian counterpart is called the Canadian Congress of Labor.

Language retention

English is the most common language in the United States and Canada, followed by Spanish in the United States and French in Canada. To understand the issue of ethnic language retention, two vital factors should be considered. First, language remains a vital link to maintaining ethnic ties and associations. Second, when two languages are used, there are two possible outcomes for the society at large: Either both languages will remain in use, or one will become dominant and replace the other.

The multiethnic character of many North American neighborhoods often means a variety of languages are used in a single area. Languages used by the fewest number of people in the neighborhood tend to be superseded by languages with more users, even if it is not the language of the host nation. For example, a minority group living in a predominately Spanish neighborhood may choose to learn Spanish before English because it is more useful in daily life. Minority groups who use two ethnic languages, such as the Ashkenazi Jews, who speak Yiddish and Hebrew, may maintain the use of one or both ethnic languages and use English—or Spanish—as well.

The government does not maintain data pertaining to language use, bilingualism, and language maintenance. No nationwide survey has been carried out to assess ethnic language use and proficiency. Due to the variables involved, performing such a survey remains difficult, if not impossible. For example, one speaker may understand spoken Finnish perfectly, but not be able to read or write the language, another might read Chinese but not speak or understand the spoken language, and a third may be able to read, write, and speak several languages, but use only one in daily life.

The Foreign-Born Population

The 1850 census was the first to collect data on the nation's foreign-born population. In 1850 there were 2.2 million people born outside the United States. By 1930 the number had risen to 14.2 million. This period of high immigration was followed by two decades of low immigration when, by 1950, the foreign-born population had dropped to 10.3 million. By 1970 the foreign-born population had declined even further to 9.6 million. Increased immigration, especially of Asian and Latin American groups, had expanded the foreign-born population to 19.8 million in 1990. By 2000 the United States had 28.4 million foreign-born

Languages and the Internet

According to a recent Internet survey, English is losing its dominance on the Web to other languages. In 2001 only 43 percent of international on-line users were native English speakers, 32 percent spoke other European languages, and 24.7 percent spoke Asian languages. In the United States, while the majority of sites remained in English, there were also a significant number of sites in Spanish. Other minority languages represented were Arabic, Chinese, French, German, Greek, Hungarian, Italian, Japanese, Korean, Polish, Portuguese, and Russian.
For more information or to view the survey data, see http://global-reach.biz/globstats/index.php3.

Chinese, Japanese, and Korean shop and business signs in Queens, New York City. Ethnic languages continue to flourish in local communities throughout North America.

NABE

The National Association for Bilingual Education (NABE) is a nonprofit organization working on behalf of limited-English-proficient (LEP) students and bilingual and English-as-a-Second-Language teachers, advocating supportive legislation and policy. Since language minority children represent 8 to 10 percent of school-age children in the United States, the NABE would like increased federal funding for the Bilingual Education Act, as well as new programs to serve LEP students. They also work to support the rights of language minority students and teachers in the public education system. For more information see http://www.nabe.org.

residents: 51 percent from Latin America, 25.5 percent from Asia, 15.3 percent from Europe, and 8.1 percent from other regions of the world.

A study of the foreign-born population may serve as the only way to discover the number of people who speak a native or ethnic language. The United States Census Bureau reported that in 2000, 5 percent of all school-age children spoke a language other than English at home (6.7 million) or had difficulty in speaking English (2.4 million)—double the rate of 20 years ago. Hispanic children had the highest rate among the ethnic groups surveyed, with 73.9 percent speaking a language other than English at home.

Of the 15.4 million people in the United States who speak another language at home, 11.2 million speak Indo-European languages. Over 8.7 million of those using Indo-European languages speak a Romance language, 690,339 speak Germanic languages, 663,450 speak Slavic languages, and 479,468 speak Indic languages. Another 3.6 million people use Asian or Pacific Island languages—over a million people in the United States speak Chinese, over half a million speak Korean, almost 800,000 speak a Philippine language, and over 400,000 speak Vietnamese. Nearly 400,000 people in America speak Semitic languages, such as Arabic, Hebrew, and others. For more detailed information see the table on page 43.

Ethnic Language Retention

Many ethnic minorities adopt the language of their host nation to better assimilate into society. However, more people continue to use their ethnic language if their community is self-sufficient, with a net-work of schools, stores, and services available in their own language.

Historically, the United States has passed laws restricting the use of ethnic languages or forcing immigrants to adopt English. Many of the laws have been overturned, but society still expects some proficiency in English in order to work, go to school, and perform daily tasks. Other factors may force immigrants to adopt English, such as the need to interact with people who do not speak their ethnic language. Social mobility and disruption of the traditional home and authority structure can also encourage people to use English.

In spite of these powerful social forces, some groups do maintain ethnic language use. Some religious groups, such as the Amish and Hutterites, continue to use German, their mother tongue, on a daily basis. Other groups, such as Native Americans, use their native tongues to

Former Vice President Al Gore speaking in Spanish to a class at an elementary school in Phoenix, Arizona, in 1999. Spanish is now the second most widely spoken language in the United States.

This table shows the languages spoken at home by the U.S. population aged five years and over in 2000 (source: U.S. Census Bureau)			
Language	**Number of speakers**	**Language**	**Number of speakers**
English only	215,423,557	Japanese	477,997
Non-English languages for which		Dravidian languages: Malayalam, Telugu,	398,434
data is available	46,951,595	Tamil; Turkish	
		(classed as Other Asian languages)	
Indo-European languages	38,119,041	Chamorro, Hawaiian, Ilocano,	313,841
Spanish or Spanish Creole	28,101,052	Indonesian, Samoan	
French	1,643,838	(classed as Other Pacific Island	
German	1,383,442	languages)	
Italian	1,008,370	Mon-Khmer, Cambodian	181,889
Russian	706,242	Miao, Hmong	168,063
Polish	667,414	Laotian	149,303
Portuguese or Portuguese Creole	564,630	Thai	120,464
French Creole	453,368		
Bengali, Marathi, Punjabi, Romany	439,289	Other languages	1,872,489
(classed as Other Indic languages)		Arabic	614,582
Greek	365,436	Amharic, Ibo, Twi, Yoruba, Bantu, Swahili	418,505
Albanian, Gaelic, Lithuanian, Romanian	327,946	(classed as African languages)	
(classed as Other Indo-European		Apache, Cherokee, Choctaw, Dakota,	203,466
languages)		Keres, Pima, Yupik	
Hindi	317,057	(classed as Other Native North	
Persian	312,085	American languages)	
Czech, Slovak, Ukrainian	301,079	Hebrew	195,374
(classed as Slavic languages)		Navajo	178,014
Urdu	262,900	Other and unspecified languages	144,575
Dutch, Pennsylvania Dutch, Afrikaans	251,135	Hungarian	117,973
(classed as West Germanic			
languages)			
Gujarati	235,988		
Serbo-Croatian	233,865		
Armenian	202,708		
Yiddish	178,945		
Danish, Norwegian, Swedish	162,252		
(classed as Scandinavian languages)			
Asian and Pacific Island languages	6,960,065		
Chinese	2,022,143		
Tagalog	1,224,241		
Vietnamese	1,009,627		
Korean	894,063		

What is a creole language?

A creole is a new language evolved from two established languages. For example, the creole spoken in southern Louisiana is a blend of pidginized French and English.

Haitian Americans listen to a Creole language local radio broadcast in Miami, Florida. Haitian Creole is a mixture of French and African languages.

Official and indigenous languages function side by side at this fast food restaurant in Tulsa, Oklahoma, where the menu is listed in both English and Cherokee.

maintain their ethnic identity. Since they form a significant portion of American society, Spanish speakers also enjoy widespread support from Mexican Americans, Puerto Ricans, Cubans, and others to maintain their language.

Indigenous Language Retention

Native American languages are the only indigenous languages of the Americas. English and Spanish were imposed on the native peoples through conquest, large-scale displacement, and immigration. Of the 175 indigenous languages surviving in the United States, only 20 languages (about 10 percent) have speakers who learned the language as children. According to the 2000 Census, 312,000 people claim to speak an indigenous language at home. The loss of indigenous languages due to English-only education and outside influences is devastating. Unlike other ethnic languages, if an indigenous language is lost in its homeland, the mother tongue itself is destroyed and almost certainly cannot be revived. Efforts among native populations to save their languages usually involve education and cultural renewal programs.

The survival of indigenous languages in the Americas is the result of several factors. First, the size of native group is important. Native Americans in Mexico, such as the Aztecs and Mayas, have been able to preserve and promote their languages due to the large number of native language speakers (over a million Aztecs and over 750,000 Mayas). Second, the length of time since the language was spoken by a large number of people and the penalties involved in speaking it are vital to language survival. Many indigenous peoples were forbidden to speak their languages and forced to adopt English or Spanish as children. The longer these policies were enforced, the less likely it is that fluent speakers have survived. From the 1880s to the 1960s the government forced Navajo and many other native children into English-only boarding schools, intending to destroy their native heritage. Thanks to modern revitalization movements, some of these groups have been able to renew their native languages.

Teaching the indigenous language is a multistep process with several challenges. First, fluent speakers need to be found. Then, a writing system or way of symbolically transmitting the language needs to be created, since many indigenous languages were only spoken, not written. Finally, a group of people needs to be taught to speak, read, and write in the language. Native peoples throughout North America are successfully implementing these steps and retaining or revitalizing their languages. Today, English and increasingly Spanish are the key languages used in schools and the workplace, so they have a survival advantage over languages that are used only at home or within a small group. For indigenous peoples use of the adopted language often leads to other cultural changes, such as in family structure and religion. Bilingualism is often the only answer for indigenous language speakers, with the native language spoken at home and English or Spanish used outside the domestic sphere.

Three generations of a Chinese American family enjoy a typical meal together. Ethnic languages and cultures continue to thrive in the home, while English is used in the wider community.

Supporting Ethnic Language Use

The survival of ethnic languages in the United States can be attributed in part to the self-sufficiency of immigrant settlements and in part to institutions that encourage ethnic language retention. Self-sufficient Mexican communities have supported the use of Spanish in the Southwest, as have Japanese communities in Hawaii and European communities in the northeastern states.

Ethnic media (newspapers, TV, radio), schools, and religious or social organizations support and promote language retention among immigrants and encourage subsequent generations to become proficient in the native tongue. While the media may help the immigrant community maintain contact with the homeland and its culture, language is more commonly promoted by personal relationships, such as teacher-student, cleric-parishioner, shopkeeper-customer, and so on.

For many indigenous language groups the focus is on education. Organizations such as the American Indian Language Development Institute work to create indigenous literatures and school curricula, even offering summer classes, university credit, and bilingual endorsements for students. Many indigenous groups have organized primary and secondary education in the native language, such as the Hawaiians, the Navajo, the Lower Kuskokwim, the Lakota, and others. Several universities now offer indigenous language programs as well, including a Lakota language program, classes in basic to advanced Navajo language and Navajo philosophy, and undergraduate and graduate programs in Hawaiian. The University of Hawaii also has a curriculum development center and a teacher enhancement program that shows teachers now to teach science, mathematics, music, and computer studies in Hawaiian.

Linguistic diversity in California

The high number of immigrants who settle in California has challenged the California Public School System. A quarter of students in California public schools are "limited-English-proficient" (LEP); 37 percent of students are native speakers of a language other than English; and 30 percent are native Spanish speakers or are bilingual in Spanish and English. For more information see http://www.cde.ca.gov/demographics/reports/COUNTY/LEP20C98.HTM.

See also

• Linguistic groups (Volume 6)
• Literacy (Volume 6)

The Hmong farmers' market in Minneapolis. The small market is run mostly by Hmong farmers who migrated to the United States after the Vietnam War (1955–1975).

Laotians include mainly two distinct groups, the Lao and the Hmong. The Lao and the Hmong are two of the fastest growing groups of Asian origin in the United States. The Lao population increased from 147,375 in 1990 to 171,937 in 2000. The Hmong are a tribal hill people mostly from northern Laos, as well as northern parts of Myanmar (formerly Burma), Thailand, Vietnam, and southern parts of China. They have different origins and speak a different language. Their population grew from 94,439 in 1990 to 169,428 in 2000. Both the Lao and Hmong communities are concentrated in California, Minnesota, Wisconsin, and North Carolina. Laos has an agrarian society based on agriculture. Most Lao and Hmong are poor and have not had any form of traditional Western education. The majority of Laotians come to the United States as refugees.

Lao and Hmong

Lao and Hmong are often categorized together, although they have different cultures and histories. The two groups, however, came to the United States under similar conditions at the end of the Vietnam War in 1975. By 1980, after overseas journeys and temporary stays in refugee camps in various countries, many refugees from Laos settled in the United States. The Hmong, unlike the Lao, originated in southwestern China. After thousands of years of Chinese domination the Hmong, under political persecution, migrated in the early 19th century to mainland Southeast Asia, where they settled in the mountainous regions of northern Myanmar, Thailand, Laos, and Vietnam.

Laos is a small landlocked country in mainland Southeast Asia. Throughout history it has been repeatedly invaded. In the first half of the 20th century Laos was ruled by the French and the Japanese. In 1949 it gained its independence. The United States was actively involved in Laos during the Vietnam War (1955–1975). In 1960 the CIA enlisted Hmong support to fight against Vietnamese communists. In return for Hmong assistance the United States provided arms, training, and food, and also promised that if the Hmong suffered defeat, it would help find them a new home. Later Laos was secretly bombed by the United States in an attempt to attack communist bases. For six years from May 1964 over two million tons of bombs were dropped on Laos, resulting in numerous civilian casualties and the destruction of villages.

Immigration to the United States

Unlike the Vietnamese, Laotians were not immediately allowed into the United States. Finally, in December 1975, 3,466 Hmong were admitted. In May 1976 another 11,000 Lao were granted entry. Slowly over the years, more

Laotians were able to resettle in the United States. The adjustment for the Hmong was particularly difficult because not only did few of them speak English, but they were also illiterate in their own language, which traditionally had been spoken and not written down. Most Hmong had been farmers and so lacked the required skills to find new employment.

The American Experience

Life in the United States is very different from what Laotians had been used to in their native country. Hmong, accustomed to sharing resources through their extended family, or clans, can no longer live that way because they are dispersed throughout the United States. Clan elders can no longer perform traditional "baby-naming" ceremonies that involve the sacrificing of chickens, pigs, or cows. In traditional Hmong society women were responsible for childbearing and domestic duties. They had to obey men in every aspect of life. In the United States Hmong women have gained equality, and wife beating and polygamy (having more than one wife) are no longer permitted. Although many Hmong have converted to Christianity, almost all continue to practice some form of Hmong tradition, such as animism, which includes a strong belief in spirits and the supernatural world. Contact with the spirit world is made through a shaman—a religious and medical leader.

Festivals

Laotian festivals revolve around year-round Buddhist traditions. The most important events are the Lao New Year Festival on April 13–16; the Boun That Luang festival celebrated during full moon in November; and the Boun Bang Fai, or Rocket Festival, in May. For Hmong the most important holiday is New Year in December, the time when the rice has been harvested, and the moon is at its darkest.

See also

- Cambodians (Volume 2)
- Koreans (Volume 6)
- Thais (Volume 10)
- Vietnamese (Volume 10)

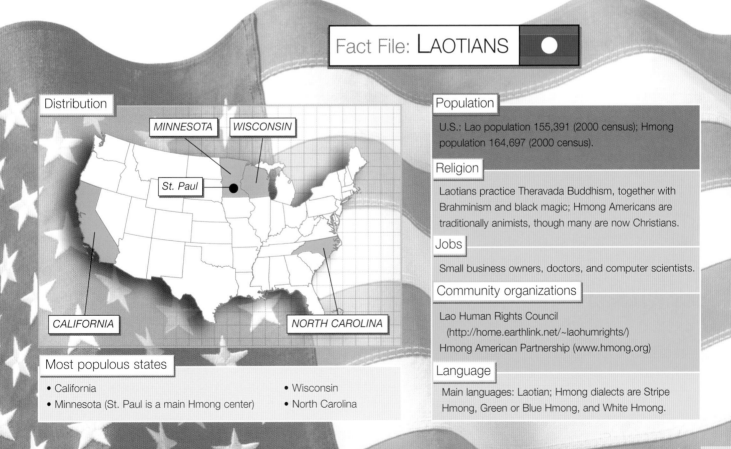

Fact File: LAOTIANS

Distribution

MINNESOTA WISCONSIN

St. Paul

CALIFORNIA NORTH CAROLINA

Most populous states

- California
- Minnesota (St. Paul is a main Hmong center)
- Wisconsin
- North Carolina

Population

U.S.: Lao population 155,391 (2000 census); Hmong population 164,697 (2000 census).

Religion

Laotians practice Theravada Buddhism, together with Brahminism and black magic; Hmong Americans are traditionally animists, though many are now Christians.

Jobs

Small business owners, doctors, and computer scientists.

Community organizations

Lao Human Rights Council
  (http://home.earthlink.net/~laohumrights/)
Hmong American Partnership (www.hmong.org)

Language

Main languages: Laotian; Hmong dialects are Stripe Hmong, Green or Blue Hmong, and White Hmong.

Useful websites

The American Latvian Association
in the United States
(www.alausa.org)
The American Latvian Youth
Association (www.alja.org)
Latvian history
(www.latvians.com)

Latvian culture

A number of Latvian cultural traditions are still practiced by Latvian Americans. At Easter eggs are colored by wrapping onion skins around uncooked eggs and then boiling them, rather than painting them. At Christmas poetry is read before gifts are opened. An important holiday among the Latvian population is Midsummer's Eve, on which a feast is prepared, houses are decorated with oak leaves and flowers, and celebrations take place for several days, including bonfires and singing. Common wedding decorations are knitted mittens and socks, following the tradition of the bride-to-be creating a dowry by knitting intricate socks and mittens.

Latvia is located on the Baltic coast of northern Europe. For most of its history it has been ruled by foreign powers. When the first Latvian immigrants arrived in North America in the 17th century, the area that makes up present-day Latvia was ruled by the Swedish (northern Latvia) and by the Polish and Lithuanians (eastern Latvia). A small province in western Latvia was mostly independent and established small colonies in Gambia (western Africa) and Tobago (an island in the Caribbean Sea).

Waves of Immigration

The earliest immigrants to North America arrived in Delaware in the 1630s, along with groups of Swedes, Finns, and Estonians. A few decades later Latvians arrived from Tobago, settling in Boston. Latvia then came under the control of Russia in the early 1720s. Throughout the 18th and 19th centuries groups of Latvians continued to migrate to North America, both in search of work and to escape repression. Small communities developed in Roxbury, Massachusetts, and in Lincoln County, Wisconsin, while others grew up in Seattle, Washington, and San Francisco, California. Due to the small number of Latvians these communities did not develop a significant Latvian identity.

After the failure of an attempted revolution in Latvia in 1905 another small wave of immigrants came to the United States, mainly a number of political leaders. Some of them returned to Latvia when independence was achieved in 1918.

The largest wave of immigration followed World War II (1939–1945), when Latvia was annexed by the Soviet Union. Almost 240,000 Latvian refugees fled the country, about 40,000 of whom eventually traveled to the United States with many others going to

A Latvian folk musician performing in a traditional western Latvian costume. Despite long periods of foreign occupation, Latvians have maintained a distinct culture.

Canada. The new immigrants mainly settled in the cities of Toronto, New York, Chicago, Philadelphia, and Boston. Within a few years social and cultural organizations developed to serve these Latvian communities, including schools, banks, choirs, dance and theater groups, churches, and political organizations.

Among Latvian Americans there is a strong interest in preserving Latvian culture and retaining ties with the country of Latvia, which regained its independence from the Soviet Union in 1991. During the occupation of Latvia by the Soviet Union there was a program of "Russification" of the Latvian population, a policy that was resented by Latvian Americans. Many Russians migrated to Latvia, and many Latvians were forced to move to other parts of the Soviet Union. By the time that Latvia became independent, only 52 percent of the population was ethnically Latvian. Russians made up 30 percent of the population, with the remainder from other Soviet republics.

Latvian Americans have tried to preserve their culture through the establishment of Latvian-language schools and churches. During the Cold War many Latvian immigrants in the United States supported the movement for an independent Latvia. Following Latvian independence, almost 9,000 Latvian Americans were granted dual American and Latvian citizenship.

Latvian festivals

St. John's Eve/Midsummer Eve (June 24—celebrated in Latvia with an official three-day holiday).
Labor Day (May 1).
Proclamation of the Republic of Latvia Day (November 18).
Christmas Day (December 25)

See also

- Emigrés and refugees (Volume 4)
- Estonians (Volume 4)
- Lithuanians (Volume 6)
- Russians (Volume 9)
- World War II (Volume 10)

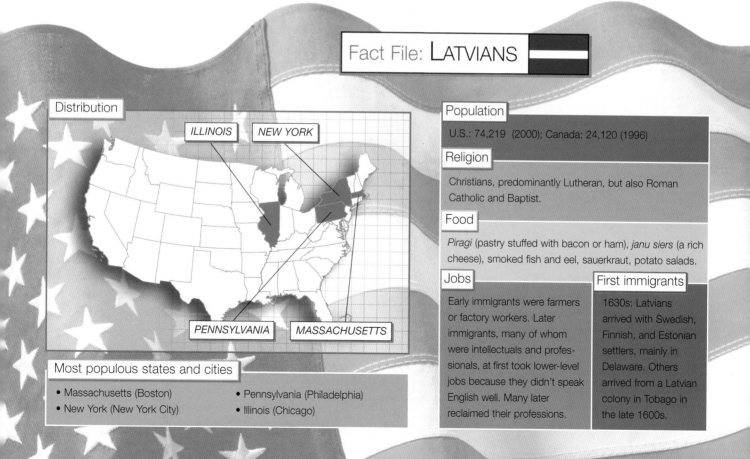

Fact File: LATVIANS

Distribution

ILLINOIS NEW YORK PENNSYLVANIA MASSACHUSETTS

Most populous states and cities

- Massachusetts (Boston)
- New York (New York City)
- Pennsylvania (Philadelphia)
- Illinois (Chicago)

Population

U.S.: 74,219 (2000); Canada: 24,120 (1996)

Religion

Christians, predominantly Lutheran, but also Roman Catholic and Baptist.

Food

Piragi (pastry stuffed with bacon or ham), janu siers (a rich cheese), smoked fish and eel, sauerkraut, potato salads.

Jobs

Early immigrants were farmers or factory workers. Later immigrants, many of whom were intellectuals and professionals, at first took lower-level jobs because they didn't speak English well. Many later reclaimed their professions.

First immigrants

1630s: Latvians arrived with Swedish, Finnish, and Estonian settlers, mainly in Delaware. Others arrived from a Latvian colony in Tobago in the late 1600s.

Lebanese

Early Lebanese immigrants settled in the northeastern states, principally New York, Massachusetts, Michigan, and Pennsylvania. More recent immigrants have settled all over the continent. Lebanese Americans are now distributed fairly evenly throughout the Northeast, the Midwest, and the South, with significant communities in, for example, Los Angeles, Houston, and New Orleans. In Canada the largest Lebanese communities are found in Montreal, Toronto, and Ottawa.

A ruined street in Beirut, Lebanon, during the civil war that lasted from 1975 until 1990. As a result of widespread fighting throughout the region, nearly a million Lebanese emigrated.

History of Lebanon

In the 19th century the area around Mount Lebanon in the eastern Mediterranean was known as Greater Syria. Greater Syria was part of the Turkish Ottoman Empire until the end of World War I (1914–1918), when the area came under French protection. Only after World War II (1939–1945) was the independent Republic of Lebanon recognized. Lebanon's long history of conquest has resulted in an ethnically and religiously diverse nation. The population is mostly Arab, with a small Armenian minority and a large number of Palestinian refugees displaced after the creation of Israel. Dominant religions include Islam (Sunni and Shi'ite), Christianity (Maronite, Melkite Catholic, Eastern Orthodox, and other sects), Muwahiddun (Druze), and Judaism.

The first Arab immigrants to settle in North America in large numbers were Christians from Syria and Lebanon, who began to arrive in the late 1800s. Violent attacks on Christians during the 1860s and political repression under the Ottomans led many to emigrate. By 1920 there were about 50,000 people of Syrian-Lebanese descent living in the United States. Few Muslims participated in this early immigration, fearing persecution as a religious minority in America.

The first wave of immigration consisted mainly of young men who settled in poor neighborhoods such as in Brooklyn, New York, and opened small stores specializing in groceries, clothing, and dry goods. Although these men had little education, their traditional value system, which emphasized hard work and self-sufficiency, led to financial success. Once established, the men returned to Lebanon to bring over their families or to find brides. Lebanese Christians typically attended Roman Catholic and Episcopalian churches.

The second wave of immigration began in the 1970s. A civil war in Lebanon from 1975 until 1990 forced nearly a million Lebanese to emigrate. While earlier Lebanese immigrants were predominantly

Notable Lebanese Americans

Paul Anka, singer.
John Arab, opera singer.
Yasmine Bleeth, actress.
Michael DeBakey, heart surgeon.
Doug Flutie, quarterback.
Khalil Gibran, poet and artist.
Philip Habib, ambassador and
  presidential envoy.
Philip Hitti, historian.
Walee Howrani, musician, pianist.
  and composer.
Norma Kamali, fashion designer.
Casey Kasem, radio show host.
Ralph Nader, politician, consumer
  advocate.
Donna Shalala, Secretary of Health,
  Education and Welfare.
Danny Thomas, comedian, founder
  of St. Jude's Hospital.
Frank Zappa, musician.

Christian, the more recent wave of arrivals included many Muslims. Those who came during the 1970s and 1980s tended to consist of entire families, who settled throughout North America. By 2000 there were about 400,000 people of Lebanese descent living in the United States. In general, later immigrants have been better educated and had a good knowledge of English, leading to rapid assimilation. Their skills as entrepreneurs have led to economic success.

Lebanese Traditions

Lebanese Americans retain notable aspects of traditional Lebanese life, such as a preference for Middle Eastern foods. The traditional lifestyle of the Lebanese revolves around the family and entertaining guests in the home. The family functions as a close-knit unit, providing mutual support and guidance. The majority of the first American-born generation married within the Lebanese community, but ethnic intermarriage is now widely accepted.

Majrajans (festivals and picnics) and *haflis* (dinner dances) are organized by Lebanese American social organizations. Children are taught the national dance, the *dabke*, while belly dancing is common at weddings. Recent immigrants have revived the use of the Arabic language in everyday life, business, and religion.

Community organizations

Canadian Arab Federation
(www.caf.ca)
Lebanese American Association
(www.laa.org)

See also

• Arab Americans (Volume 1)
• Israelis (Volume 6)
• Palestinians (Volume 8)
• Syrians (Volume 10)

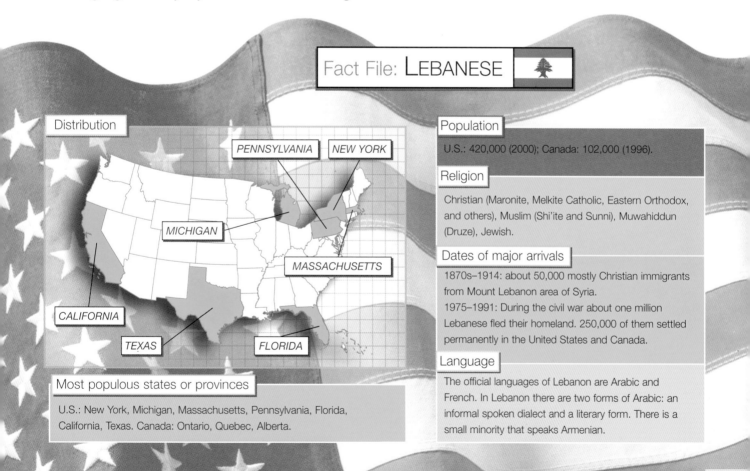

Fact File: LEBANESE

Distribution

PENNSYLVANIA   NEW YORK

MICHIGAN

MASSACHUSETTS

CALIFORNIA

TEXAS   FLORIDA

Most populous states or provinces

U.S.: New York, Michigan, Massachusetts, Pennsylvania, Florida, California, Texas. Canada: Ontario, Quebec, Alberta.

Population

U.S.: 420,000 (2000); Canada: 102,000 (1996).

Religion

Christian (Maronite, Melkite Catholic, Eastern Orthodox, and others), Muslim (Shi'ite and Sunni), Muwahiddun (Druze), Jewish.

Dates of major arrivals

1870s–1914: about 50,000 mostly Christian immigrants from Mount Lebanon area of Syria.
1975–1991: During the civil war about one million Lebanese fled their homeland. 250,000 of them settled permanently in the United States and Canada.

Language

The official languages of Lebanon are Arabic and French. In Lebanon there are two forms of Arabic: an informal spoken dialect and a literary form. There is a small minority that speaks Armenian.

Liberians

Located on the west coast of Africa, Liberia—meaning "place of freedom" in Latin—has a highly unusual history. For most of the country's history people emigrated from North America to Liberia rather than the other way around. Early in the 19th century North American political and religious groups established Liberia as a place where freed African American slaves could return to Africa. The American Colonization Society bought land from West African tribes in 1821, and from 1822 until the end of the Civil War in 1865 nearly 15,000 African Americans resettled in Liberia.

Liberian Ethnic Groups

Known as Americo-Liberians, the African Americans who resettled Liberia made up only about 1 percent of the population, but they became the ruling class when Liberia declared its independence in 1847. The majority of the Liberian population was composed of a large number of African ethnic groups, most notably the Kpelle, Bassa, Gio, Kru, Grebo, and Mano. English is the official language, but at least 29 other languages exist as well.

Liberia's Unsettled Political History

Liberians first modeled their government on that of the United States, but the country was economically and militarily weak. In the late 19th century Liberia lost large portions of its land to France and Britain. Economic stability was finally achieved in 1926, when the Firestone Tire & Rubber Company leased large areas of Liberia for rubber production. Corruption dominated the Liberian government until William V. S. Tubman was elected president in 1944, and the country began to prosper. After Tubman's death W. R. Tolbert was elected president in 1972, but he was assassinated in a coup in 1980.

A long period of dictatorship began. Civil war broke out in 1989, and a rebel group led by Charles Taylor took over the government in 1990. The war continued until 1997, during which time nearly one-third of the Liberian population left the country, and many thousands were killed. Liberian citizens elected Taylor in a new government in 1997; but while some citizens returned, instability in Liberia continues, with many restrictions placed on its citizens.

Throughout the 1990s many Liberians fled to North America to avoid the civil war. The United States Immigration and Naturalization Service (INS) reported that 13,458 Liberians entered the country

African Americans departing from Savannah, Georgia, for Liberia on the steamship Laurada *in 1896. Freed African American slaves were encouraged to resettle in Liberia.*

between 1990 and 1997. Thousands more received Temporary Protective Status (TPS) from the INS, which was revoked following the 1997 elections in Liberia. Liberian Americans closely follow the political situation in both the United States and Liberia. Despite the democratic elections of the 1990s, Liberian Americans continue to lobby the government to grant permanent status to all the Liberians who were given Temporary Protective Status in the 1990s.

Cultural Traditions

Liberian Americans differ from Liberians in that nearly all of them speak English, while only 20 percent of the Liberian population consider English to be their first language. Also, the majority of Liberian Americans are Christian, while Christians number only 10 percent of the population in Liberia.

Liberian American gatherings such as birthdays, funerals, and most holidays are similar to those of African Americans. Liberian American weddings have both African and North American influences: The bridal party attends the Christian ceremony wearing colorful Liberian dress, and traditional drummers often provide music. Liberian Americans share the Liberian love of soccer, and a soccer match is usually part of any Liberian American social gathering.

George Weah

Born in Monrovia, Liberia, and currently living in New York, George Weah is a world-renowned soccer player. In 1995 Weah held the titles of FIFA World Player of the Year, European Player of the Year, and African Player of the Year. Weah's generous support of his home country has inspired Liberians and Liberian Americans alike.

See also

- African Americans (Volume 1)
- African Canadians (Volume 1)
- Slavery (Volume 9)
- West Africans (Volume 10)

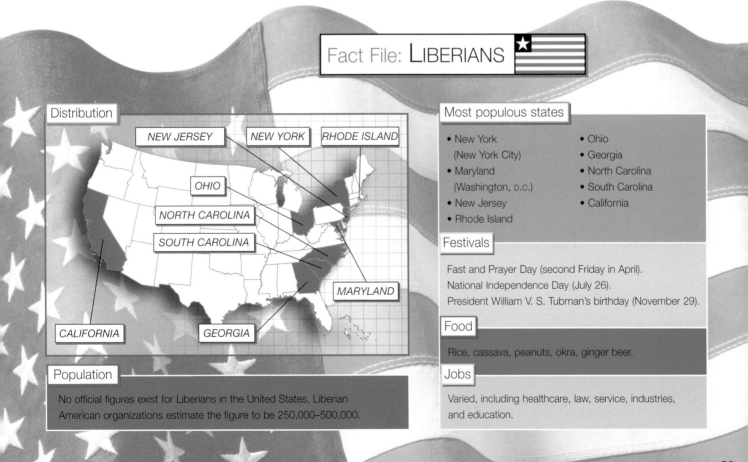

Fact File: LIBERIANS

Distribution

NEW JERSEY
NEW YORK
RHODE ISLAND
OHIO
NORTH CAROLINA
SOUTH CAROLINA
MARYLAND
CALIFORNIA
GEORGIA

Most populous states

- New York (New York City)
- Maryland (Washington, D.C.)
- New Jersey
- Rhode Island
- Ohio
- Georgia
- North Carolina
- South Carolina
- California

Festivals

Fast and Prayer Day (second Friday in April).
National Independence Day (July 26).
President William V. S. Tubman's birthday (November 29).

Food

Rice, cassava, peanuts, okra, ginger beer.

Population

No official figures exist for Liberians in the United States. Liberian American organizations estimate the figure to be 250,000–500,000.

Jobs

Varied, including healthcare, law, service, industries, and education.

Useful websites

U.S. Census Bureau information on language usage (http://www.census.gov/population/www/socdemo/lang_use.html)

Family education (http://www.factmonster.com)

Database showing the origin of state names (http://www.namely-yours.com/namesstates.php)

Navajo Code Talker Association (http://www.lapahie.com/NCTA.cfm)

A rare example of Native American "writing," this page of symbols comes from an Aztec syllabary in which each written character is used to represent a syllable; they are then joined to create meaningful phrases. The handwriting at the bottom was added by a Spanish scribe.

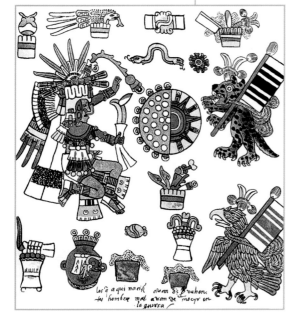

When the United States was founded in 1776, the major languages spoken daily, outside of the six major Native American linguistic family groups, were English, Dutch, French, and German. German was so common that the Articles of Confederation were published in English and German. Today the United States lists 231 national or official languages. Of these 176 are living languages, 3 are second languages without native speakers, and 52 are extinct languages. After English Spanish is the most widely spoken language in the United States, with over 17 million speakers. Canada has English and French as its official languages, and more than six million Canadians are native French speakers. The majority of French-speaking Canadians live in Quebec and are known as "Quebecois." Other French-speaking groups in North America include Acadians, also in Canada, and Cajuns, who live mainly in Louisiana and Texas.

"English Only" Movements

Movements to establish English as the official language of the United States date from 1780, when John Adams proposed to the Continental Congress that an official academy be created to "purify, develop, and dictate usage of English." This proposal was voted down because it was considered to be an infringement of personal liberty. Until the late 1800s the United States of America was tolerant of linguistic diversity.

Large numbers of eastern and southern European, as well as Asian, immigrants prompted the enactment of restrictive language laws. In order to "Americanize" immigrants, English literacy requirements were established for public employment, naturalization, immigration, and voting rights. The government forced Native American children to attend English-language boarding schools, where they were punished for speaking their native languages.

The "English Only" movement of the 1980s wanted to pass laws that restricted or prohibited the use by government agencies of languages other than English. Some states have passed "English Only" laws, but they vary. Some states have simply declared English the "official" language of the state. Others have limited or prohibited the use of other languages in bilingual programs, voting ballots, or courtroom translation. The "English Only" campaigns target mainly Hispanics and Asians, who are the majority of recent immigrants. Today about 96 percent of American residents are fluent in English; however, that leaves about 10 million residents who are not fluent in English, according to the 2000 Census.

North American Spanish

Only a small minority of North America's Spanish speakers have emigrated directly from Spain. Most have come from Central and South America, in particular from Mexico, Puerto Rico, and Cuba. Spanish has become the unofficial second language of the United States, and a huge network of Spanish-language media, from newspapers and magazines to film, television, and radio, has grown up to support this. Although there is an "official" spoken and written Spanish (Castillian), there are many dialectical differences in the languages spoken by the various immigrant groups.

Cajuns, Acadians, and Quebecois

Canada's Acadians and the United States' Cajuns are descended from the same French immigrants who first settled the region of Acadia in Canada. Many Acadians migrated south to French-owned Louisiana after their forced expulsion from Acadia by the British in 1755 and became known as "Cajuns." Despite both being rooted in French, the dialects spoken by Cajuns and Acadians have distinct differences. Due to its close association with Native Americans and other non-English-speaking groups, the Cajun language has adopted many "foreign" words. Conversely, the Acadian dialect remains closer to its original form since its speakers have remained more isolated. Acadians strive to remain distinct from Canada's main French-speaking population, the Quebecois. Living predominantly in the province of Quebec in the cities of Montreal and Quebec, these French Canadians make up almost one-fourth of Canada's total population. Despite Canada's progressive multicultural policies, many Quebecois feel that only in their province can they work and live within a French cultural environment. During the past 30 years there has been a strong movement in favor of separatism, and in 1995 the referendum to withdraw from Canada was only narrowly defeated. Today separatism support has declined but remains strong.

Studies of Native American Languages

North American linguistic studies have suffered from a lack of written records. The only written Native American languages before European contact were those of the Aztec and Maya, and few texts remain from which to develop a linguistic structure. Some Native Americans used sign language, consisting of hand or arm gestures, or smoke signals to convey information. These shared signals made it possible for Native Americans speaking different languages to communicate ideas or simple messages. Today there are not enough

Children dress in traditional Spanish costumes at the Old Spanish Days fiesta in Santa Barbara, California. This fiesta brings Hispanic and Latino children together to celebrate their shared Spanish heritage.

Ethnologue.com

This website contains one of the most comprehensive databases for the world's languages. The site includes language maps showing the locations of speakers. The online bibliography allows for searches by author, country, serial, or subject. For a complete listing of the languages used in America, the number of speakers, and the present state of the language see http://www.ethnologue.com/show_country.asp?name=USA, or to view the United States maps, go to http://www.ethnologue.com/show_map.asp?name=USA.

Languages spoken at home

This list shows the most widely spoken languages in the United States. The number in parentheses shows the number of speakers, according to the 2000 Census.

English (198,601,000)
Spanish (17,339,000)
French (1,702,000)
German (1,547,000)
Italian (1,309,000)
Chinese (1,249,000)
Tagalog (843,000)
Polish (723,000)
Korean (626,000)
Vietnamese (507,000)
Portuguese (430,000)
Japanese (428,000)
Greek (388,000)
Arabic (355,000)
Hindi (Urdu) (331,000)
Russian (242,000)
Yiddish (213,000)
Thai (Laotian) (206,000)
Persian (202,000)
French Creole (188,000)
Armenian (150,000)
Navajo (149,000)
Hungarian (148,000)
Hebrew (144,000)
Dutch (143,000)
Mon-Khmer (Cambodian) (127,000)
Gujarathi (Indian) (102,000)

people who can speak Native American languages or trained people to collect data about them, and many are becoming endangered.

Many place names and around half the state names in the United States, however, come from Native American languages. Everyday English also includes many Native American words, such as moccasin, moose, raccoon, skunk, terrapin, tomahawk, totem, and wampum. Several English words, including chocolate, coyote, and tomato, come from various Mexican languages, and words such as barbecue, cannibal, hurricane, maize, and potato originate from Native American languages in the West Indies.

Asia is considered the most likely origin of most Native American languages, although the link has not been proven. These languages are highly developed in variety of sounds, word order, and word choice. Many Native American languages are polysynthetic, meaning that word elements are joined together to form a composite word that functions like a sentence in English. Most Native American languages do not have gender in the same way as Indo-European languages. For

Native American state names

Alaska: From the Eskimo word *Alakshak,* meaning "great lands" or "peninsula."
Arkansas: A Quapaw name for the Arkansea or Arkansa tribe, meaning "downstream place."
Connecticut: A Native American word previously recorded as *Quinnehtukqut,* or "beside the long tidal river."
Hawaii: Origin uncertain. Possibly named after Hawaii Loa, who discovered the island, or based on a native Hawaiian word for homeland, *Owhyhee.*
Idaho: Said to have originated from the Kiowa-Apache name for the Comanche tribe (*Idahi*) or perhaps from the phrase *E Dah Hoe,* meaning "gem of the mountains."
Illinois: From an Illini or Algonquin term meaning "warriors."
Iowa: Native American for "the beautiful land" or "this is the place."
Kansas: Siouan for "people of the south wind."
Kentucky: Iroquoian words *Ken-tah-ten,* "land of tomorrow," or *Ken-ta-ke,* "meadow land."
Massachusetts: From Algonquin words meaning "great mountain place."
Michigan: From Algonquin words meaning "great water."
Minnesota: Dakotah word for "sky-blue water" or Siouan word for "water-cloudy."
Mississippi: Algonquin for "father of waters" or possibly based on Chippewa Indian words meaning "big river."
Missouri: From a Missouri Indian tribe, possibly meaning "place of the large canoes" or "big and muddy."
Nebraska: Oto or Omaha for "flat water."
North/South Dakota: From the name of the Dakotah tribe. *Dakotah* is a Sioux word meaning "allies/friends."
Ohio: Iroquoian for "great river."
Oklahoma: From Choctaw words for "red people."
Tennessee: Named after Cherokee villages—*Tanasi.* The meaning is unknown.
Texas: From a Native American word, *teyas,* meaning "friends."
Utah: Named for the Ute tribe, said to mean "people of the mountains."
Wisconsin: Possibly from the Chippewa Indian word *Ouisconsin,* meaning "grassy place."
Wyoming: Based on the Algonquin or Delaware Indian word meaning "large prairie place."

This table shows the states in the United States that have names derived from Native American languages. Information on the origin of state names can also be found at http://www.namely-yours.com/namesstates.php

example, in Algonquian languages nouns are animate or inanimate, rather than masculine or feminine.

A language family consists of two or more spoken languages that are distinct from each other yet related historically in that they are descended from a single ancestor language. All the members of the language family are closely related in terms of phonetics (sounds), grammar (word choice and word order), and vocabulary (words). Edward Sapir created the most widely accepted classification of Native American languages in 1929. He suggested six major linguistic family groups, including Eskimo-Aleut, Algonquian-Shalishan-Wakashan, Nadene, Penutian, Hokan-Siouan, and Aztec-Tanoan.

Native American Language Families

The Eskimo-Aleut language family includes Aleut and Inuktitut, spoken in the Aleutian Islands and Kodiak Peninsula of Alaska, as well as Canada, Greenland, and Siberia. Both language groups are polysynthetic—word pieces are mainly added to the end of the word unit, like a suffix in English. In earlier times Aleut and Inuktitut used pictographs (picture writing) to convey written messages. Since the 18th century they have adopted the Roman alphabet introduced by missionaries. However, in Siberia they commonly use the Cyrillic alphabet of Russia.

The most widespread Native American language family in North America was Algonquian-Shalishan-Wakashan. Today about 130,000 people in Canada and a few thousand in the United States speak one of the Algonquian-Shalishan-Wakashan languages, which include about 50 different tongues. Peoples speaking Shalishan languages live throughout British Columbia in Canada, as well as in Washington, Oregon, Idaho, and Montana in the United States. Groups speaking Wakashan languages commonly live along the Pacific Northwest coast of the United States. Like the Aleut and Inuktitut languages, the Algonquian-Shalishan-Wakashan family uses mainly suffixes to create a composite word that means the same as a whole sentence in English.

Spoken in parts of Canada and Alaska, the Nadene languages Athabascan, Haida, and Tlingit use tones to convey meaning. There is some use of suffixes to create composite words.

The Penutian languages are native to California and may be related to languages used in other parts of the Pacific Northwest coast, as well as in Mexico and parts of Central America. In many ways Penutian languages are more like English and other Indo-European languages.

The Hokan-Siouan language family is still being studied, and there is some disagreement about which languages should be included. The groups generally accepted as Hokan-Siouan are Muskogean, Caddoan, Yuman, Iroquoian, and Siouan. The Muskogean languages are spoken in Oklahoma and Florida. The Caddoan branch is found in

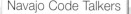
Navajo Code Talkers

Philip Johnston, the son of a Navajo missionary, came up with the idea of using Navajo speakers to transmit messages in the Pacific during World War II (1939–1945). The Navajo radio operators, called "Code Talkers" (above), used one of the most difficult Native American languages to transmit information on tactics, troop movements, orders, and other vital battlefield communications over telephones and radios. Throughout the war, between 375 and 420 Navajos served as "Code Talkers." Even after the war Navajo remained a valuable code for the Marines. For more information see www.usmc.mil/history.nsf/Table%20of%20 Contents/77f992b2acb682eb8525 64d70059c642?OpenDocument& Expand Section=8,13, or visit the National Code Talkers Association website at http://www.lapahie.com/ NCTA.cfm.

Hawaiian

The native language of Hawaii, Hawaiian, originates from Polynesia. According to the 1990 Census, there are 8,872 speakers of Hawaiian. It is the language of the entire community of one small island group; however, most Hawaiian speakers are elderly and scattered. The Hawaiian community and state government are trying to revive the language by reestablishing schools to teach it, such as the Hawaiian Studies Department and the Hale Kuamo'o Hawaiian Language Center at the University of Hawaii. Classes are also offered at the Punana Leo Hawaiian Medium Preschools and the Papahana Kaiapuni Hawai'i (Hawaiian Immersion Public Schools), at the University of Hawaii, as well as at all state community colleges.

See also

- Cajuns and Acadians (Volume 2)
- Canadians, French (Volume 2)
- Language retention (Volume 6)
- Literacy (Volume 6)
- Native Americans (Volumes 7 & 8)
- Spanish (Volume 10)

Today Native American children are taught Native American languages in an attempt to keep them from extinction. Here a teacher is instructing a class in the Aleut language.

Oklahoma and North Dakota, and the Yuman branch is spoken in Arizona and California. The Iroquoian languages are found in New York, Wisconsin, Oklahoma, and North Carolina. The final group of languages, Siouan, includes such tongues as Catawba, Winnebago, Osage, Dakota, Assiniboin, and Crow, spoken in South Carolina, Minnesota, Wisconsin, Nebraska, North Dakota, South Dakota, Montana, and Oklahoma. All Hokan-Siouan languages contain word elements with fixed meanings, which join to form composite words.

The Aztec-Tanoan languages, spoken from the northwest United States to Mexico and Central America, have two branches: Uto-Aztecan, divided into the Nahuatlan and Shoshonean tongues, and Tanoan, used in the Rio Grande Valley of Texas, New Mexico, and Arizona. The Zuñi of New Mexico may be connected to Tanoan. Like other Native American languages, the Aztec-Tanoan languages use suffixes to create a composite word that is equivalent to an English sentence.

Survival of Native American Languages

With very few exceptions the outlook for the survival of Native American languages is not good. The success of the "English Only" movements, first initiated more than two centuries ago, has resulted in the loss of many of North America's native languages, and of those that remain, most are spoken only by a small handful of elders. Some native groups are working to revitalize their languages as part of increased attention to cultural identity. These groups, including the Hawaiians, the Inuit, and others, are creating language-learning facilities, tribal classes, language camps, and school classes to ensure their languages live on. Those groups without fluent speakers are in danger of losing their languages permanently.

Literacy

Historically, literacy was defined as the ability to read and use printed materials. Today Congress defines literacy as "an individual's ability to read, write, and speak in English, and compute and solve problems at levels of proficiency necessary to function on the job and in society, to achieve one's goals, and develop one's knowledge and potential." In 1992 the National Adult Literacy Survey (NALS), conducted by the Department of Education on behalf of Congress, found that half of American adults perform at the lowest two literacy levels, 32 percent function at Level 3 literacy, 17 percent at Level 4, and 3 percent at Level 5, the highest literacy level. While 66 to 75 percent of adults at Levels 1 and 2 said they could read or write English "well" or "very well," they had trouble with higher-level reading and problem-solving skills. Approximately a quarter of those who performed at Level 1 were immigrants learning English; 38 to 43 percent of black, 54 percent of Hispanic, 30 to 36 percent of Asian, and 14 to 16 percent of white respondents scored at the lowest literacy level.

Those who scored on the lowest literacy level were more likely to be older and less educated, usually to the eighth grade or lower, and tended to be in low-level, low-paying jobs. Many were members of ethnic or racial minority groups. On average, Mexican and Central/South American adults scored lowest in the Hispanic group. Asian/Pacific Islander and Native American adults scored, on average, similarly to Hispanics. With the exception of black adults, who often had only limited educational opportunities, people born in the United States scored better than those born abroad.

The NALS found that many Americans who are literate in foreign languages were illiterate in English. The 1979 National Chicano Survey (NCS), a study of Americans of Mexican descent, estimated that of the 31.8 million Americans who speak a foreign language, approximately 17 million (54 percent) speak Spanish. In 39 states Spanish remains the most common non-English language. The NCS

Useful websites

Literacy.org
   (http://litserver.literacy.upenn.edu)
National Adult Literacy Database
   (http://www.nald.ca)
National Center for Education
   Statistics (http://nces.ed.gov/naal)
National Center for ESL Literacy
   Education (http://www.cal.org/ncle)
National Institute for Literacy
   (http://www.nifl.gov)

The English-Only laws

The first English-Only laws were passed in the late 1880s. Language-restriction laws were often enacted to decrease competition for jobs. For example, in 1897 Pennsylvania passed an English-speaking requirement for coal miners to exclude Italians and Hungarians from the mines. Early in the 20th century settlement houses and service organizations offered evening classes in English as part of attempts to "Americanize" immigrants. Many native-born Americans saw foreign languages as a sign of divided loyalties and felt immigrants should shed all traits of ethnicity, including language. During World War I (1914–1918) prejudice against Germans brought the first ban on the use of German in public. German-language newspapers, schools, cultural institutions, and churches were closed. The English-Only movement remains strong in many parts of the United States.

To help immigrants assimilate into society, adult literacy classes were held for men and women in the 1930s (left) and continue today.

Literacy in Canada

About 22 percent of Canadians age 16 years and older have serious difficulty reading printed materials. In addition, 24 to 26 percent can read only material that is simple and clearly laid out. As in Mexico and the United States, literacy levels vary by region. About 18 percent of 16-year-olds or older in the Atlantic region and 21 percent of those in Quebec have less than an eighth-grade education, compared to 12 percent of Ontarians and 11 percent of those in the western provinces.

Many radio stations broadcast in Spanish, such as KCOR in Texas.

reported that 52 percent of those surveyed were English literate, 42 percent were Spanish literate, and 22 percent were biliterate, or literate in both languages. More research is needed to update these findings, since this is the most recent biliteracy survey.

Language Diversity in North America

English, German, Dutch, French, Spanish, Italian, Portuguese, Greek, Yiddish, Arabic, and hundreds of Native American languages and creoles (a mix of two languages) were spoken in the United States in the 18th and 19th centuries. During this period most immigrants settled in rural enclaves and had native language literacy. European immigrants to the United States enjoyed far more linguistic tolerance than other groups, and school teachers taught in Swedish, Polish, Italian, German, and Czech based on the local population.

During the colonial period Germans (known as the "Pennsylvania Dutch," from the German word *Deutsch*, meaning "German") represented a third of the population of Pennsylvania and continued to arrive at a rate of 7,000 annually. Colonists feared that Germans would soon outnumber English, making German the common language. Eventually, however, German immigration declined, and the Germans adopted English; but German is still used among religious communities.

After the Louisiana Purchase of 1803 French was spoken by 85 percent of the population of that area. When Louisiana became a state in 1812, French continued to be used extensively in state government, and the legislature used French and English until the Civil War. After the war Union troops abolished French language rights to punish French speakers for their support of the Confederacy.

In California the English elite at first treated Spanish speakers, especially rich Spanish speakers, with tolerance. The 1849 constitution recognized Spanish language rights, but in 1855 the state discontinued Spanish-language schooling. English literacy requirements in California prevented many Spanish and Chinese from being able to vote. Faced with the reality of their position as second-class citizens, many immigrants and non-English speakers who wanted to climb the social ladder understood that they had to master a good grasp of English and encouraged their children to do so as well. For much of the late 19th and early 20th centuries this led to problems of cultural identity for many middle- and upper-class families who tried to hide their ethnic background. Today, remaining true to ones ethnic heritage is encouraged in most of California, as in many parts of North America, and is not as much of an obstacle to success as it was in the past. There remain, however, many issues surrounding integration and assimilation of non-English-speaking groups.

The Dominance of English

Native Americans were pressured to adopt English from the arrival of the first settlers. After the Civil War they resisted the white expansion into the West. The Indian Peace Commission of 1868 decided to pacify the Plains tribes through forced assimilation, making them conform to the dominant culture and language of the European settlers—a practice that continued until the 1960s. In the 1880s government bounty hunters were hired to kidnap Native American children and take them to boarding schools, where they were harshly punished for speaking their native languages. Native Americans have begun a cultural resurgence, promoting native languages and pride in cultural heritage. Their literacy in both English and native languages is growing in many areas.

After the Spanish-American War (1898) English was declared the "official language of the schoolroom" in Puerto Rico. The hated policy resulted in a dropout rate of 84 percent by the third grade. Few Puerto Ricans felt any need to learn English except when entering the United States to look for work. After Puerto Rico gained a measure of autonomy in 1948, Spanish was restored as the language of instruction.

Due to a compulsory schooling law and adult enthusiasm in Hawaii, the majority of Hawaiians were literate in their own language by the 1850s. In 1853 English instruction was introduced in Hawaiian schools, and by 1896 it became the only language of instruction. The United States forcibly annexed Hawaii in 1898, and in 1920 a two-tier education system was established that separated children on the basis of English proficiency. In practice it was a racial division, with whites in one school and nonwhites in another. The system was dismantled in the 1950s. Hawaiian is enjoying resurgence in popularity, and today over 8,000 Hawaiians are literate in the language.

The Immigration Act of 1917 changed immigration law so that immigrants who could not read English or some other language or dialect would not be able to enter the United States. So, the Immigration and Naturalization service began administering literacy exams. Within the country non-English-speaking groups dwindled, and native language instruction disappeared except in a handful of rural or religious schools. Non-English-speaking communities began to grow again after 1965, when racial criteria were removed from United States immigration policy. Today in California, for example, there are over 27 million residents for whom English is a second language.

Secretary of Education Rod Paige delivers a speech outlining the education policies for 2002.

See also

- Assimilation (Volume 1)
- Language retention (Volume 6)
- Linguistic groups (Volume 6)

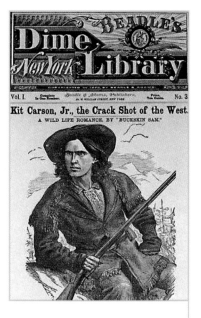

Handsome heroes and heroines looked out from the covers of "dime novels" that told romanticized stories of American life while instilling in readers "correct" moral values. Dime novels were so called because they cost 10 cents.

Early American writing was strongly influenced by English literary traditions, and voices from other immigrant groups were not commonly found in print until the 1900s. Many early American writers addressed the problems of racism, immigration, and multiculturalism that faced 19th-century American society. Some works had a profound effect on American sensibilities. *Uncle Tom's Cabin* (1852), by Harriet Beecher Stowe (1811–1896), provided a shocking insight into the practice of slavery, and some critics credit the book with sparking the Civil War of 1861. Nonfiction works, such as Jane Addams' (1860–1935) *Twenty Years at Hull House* (1910), also reported the experiences of minorities and immigrants. Addams had founded the world-famous social settlement Hull House on Chicago's Near West Side in 1889. From Hull House, where she lived and worked until her death in 1935, she built her reputation as the country's most prominent woman through her writing, her settlement work, and her international efforts for world peace. She became a focus for social change on a large scale.

A Literature for Immigrants

There were few publications for immigrants before the 1860s. *Malaeska*, the first "dime novel," was published in 1860. Aimed at the young urban working class, it told of a beautiful Indian maiden who married a white settler. It sold 65,000 copies within months, and its success prompted publishers to produce a novel a week. Dime novels' hidden social motive was to instill American values into the new immigrant groups; fictional young heroes and heroines faced moral dilemmas but ultimately made the "right" choices. The stories reinforced the preferred values of the growing industrial society—hard work and honesty being among the most important. Stock characters from these novels, such as the honest cowboy, the Western heroine, the noble Indian, the romantic young couple, and the evil villain, formed the basis for stories for the next century. The characters were not always fictional, since dime novels often recounted real-life stories, from Western showman Buffalo Bill to athlete Frank Meriwell. However, such biographies were often embellished for the sake of moral clarity.

Poets with a Purpose

The 19th century produced a number of influential poets, including Henry Wadsworth Longfellow (1807–1882), who often used cultural conflict to make a moral point. For example, in *Evangeline* (1847) French Canadian lovers are separated when the British expelled Acadians from Nova Scotia, and in *Song of Hiawatha* (1855) a Chippewa Native American teaches peace between natives and whites.

Another major American literary figure of the 19th century was the poet Walt Whitman (1819–1892). His *Leaves of Grass* (1855) described

---

Great novelists

North America has produced a number of novelists whose works rank alongside the best in world literature. Writers such as Nathaniel Hawthorne, Edith Wharton, F. Scott Fitzgerald, William Faulkner, Ernest Hemingway, Stephen Crane, John Dos Passos, Thomas Wolfe, Robertson Davies, Gore Vidal, Margaret Atwood, and Tom Wolfe have all produced novels of originality and power, and it seems likely that the North American novel will continue to be a source of influence well into the future.

and praised the common man, local immigrants, and ethnic groups such as African Americans and Native Americans (whom he called "red aborigines"), and expressed Whitman's belief that American ideals might serve as an example to the world. He influenced the next generation of poets and writers, including Carl Sandburg (1878–1967), whose poems praised industrial America.

Portraying Native Americans

Native Americans were consistently stereotyped in literature either as good "noble savages" or as evil "red devils" without culture or morals. While some authors wrote with sympathy, others penned "true" but distorted tales; anthropologists and folklorists visited reservations but wrote histories and biographies that were often colored by misinterpretation and half-truths. Among the first and best known writers on Native American themes was James Fenimore Cooper (1789–1851). He romanticized Native Americans and the West and was the first to portray the Indian as a "noble savage" in *The Last of the Mohicans* (1826). It was not until the 1960s that Native Americans began their own literary revival to redress over 100 years of imbalance.

Two nonfiction works that portray the Native American perspective stand out. The first, *Black Elk Speaks* (1932), by John G. Neihardt (1881–1973), has become a classic source on 19th-century Plains Indian culture. The second, Dee Brown's (1908–2002) *Bury My Heart at Wounded Knee*, is a fully documented account of the systematic destruction of the Native American way of life during the late 19th century. Published in 1971, it brought a reaction from reviewers and the reading public alike of first shock and then a deep sense of shame. It went on to sell over five million copies in 15 languages; it remains in print.

Writers from minority groups

Writers from minority groups have written for several reasons: to record the history and traditions of their people; to show the effects of the loss or the recovery of heritage and the individual's search for true self; to expose race, gender, and class prejudice in America; to show the blending and clashing of cultures within American society; or to speak out for social and political change. However, some immigrant or minority authors—such as the Russian-born novelist Vladimir Nabokov (1899–1977)—were more concerned with individuals and characters than with politics.

The Last of the Mohicans, *written by James Fenimore Cooper, was one of the first novels to feature Native Americans in central, positive roles. In 1992 the novel was made into an Academy Award-winning film starring Daniel Day Lewis, who played the main character Hawkeye (center), a scout.*

Famous immigrant writers

Bharati Mukherjee (1940–), naturalized Canadian portraying Indian immigrants' and women's experience. *Tiger's Daughter* (!972), *Wife* (1975), *Jasmine* (1989), *Holder of the World* (1993), *Leave It to Me* (1997).

Mario Puzo (1920–1979), Italian American contemporary novelist. *The Fortunate Pilgrim* (1964), *The Godfather* (1969).

Arnold R. Rojas (1899–1988), Mexican American writer who helped create 1960s ethnic pride. *California Vaqueros* (1953), *Vaqueros and Buckaroos* (1979),

William Saroyan (1908–1981), Armenian American novelist and playwright drawing on immigrant culture. *Time of Your Life* (1939, Pulitzer Prize for Literature), *My Name Is Aram* (1940), *The Human Comedy* (1942).

Amy Tan (1952–) (below), Chinese American novelist dealing with Chinese American women. *Joy Luck Club* (1989), *Kitchen God's Wife* (1991), *The Hundred Secret Senses* (1995), *The Bonesetter's Daughter* (2001).

African Americans in Literature

The first literature to deal with African American themes was written about slavery and racism in the Southern states before the Civil War. *Uncle Tom's Cabin*, Harriet Beecher Stowe's literary landmark of 1852, was a thinly veiled sentimental novel exposing the evils of slavery. Another of America's greatest novels is *Huckleberry Finn* (1884), by Mark Twain (Samuel L. Clemens, 1835–1910), in which the negative Southern attitude toward African American slaves underlies the adventures of Huck and Jim, a black runaway slave, whom Huck eventually recognizes as his equal and friend.

Black–white relations were still an issue when Harper Lee (1926–) wrote *To Kill a Mockingbird* in 1960. A six-year-old narrator tells the story of her father, a small-town Southern lawyer who suffers for his integrity when he defends a black man accused of the rape of a white woman. The book won the 1961 Pulitzer Prize for fiction.

African American authors have made a great contribution to American literature. The orator and writer Frederick Douglass (1817–1895) started life as a slave and later became a newspaper editor and a consultant to President Abraham Lincoln. His autobiography, *The Life and Times of Frederick Douglass* (1882), is a classic of American literature.

W.E.B. Du Bois (1868–1963), another major literary figure, was probably the most important black protest leader of the first half of the 20th century. He conducted the first studies of a black American community, *Philadelphia Negro: A Social Study*, in 1899. His support of black literature, culture, and art made him an important element in the reawakening of black identity in 20th-century America.

Other notable black American writers include the poet Langston Hughes (1902–1967), one of most influential of early African Americans whose jazzlike poems helped herald the Harlem Renaissance. James Baldwin's (1924–1987) personal nonfiction, particularly *Go Tell It on the Mountain* (1953), was an indictment of American society for its discrimination against African Americans. More recently, Toni Morrison (1931–) has become a popular novelist with a special focus on black women. Her major works include *Bluest Eye* (1969), *Sula* (1973), *Song of Solomon* (1977), and *Beloved* (1987), a Pulitzer Prize-winning tragedy of slavery and its aftereffects. Morrison was awarded the Nobel Prize for Literature in 1993. In 1982 Alice Walker (1944–), a black writer, novelist, poet, and essayist, published *The Color Purple*, which tells the story of Celie, a young black woman growing up in the South. The book won the Pulitzer Prize for Literature in 1983. In 1985 it was made into a much-praised film.

Jewish American Writers

The Jewish community has produced another group of influential writers in North America. Isaac Bashevis Singer (1904–), a Yiddish novelist, critic, and journalist, produced fablelike stories written in Yiddish. *The Family Moskat* (1950), one of his best-known works, focuses on the decline of traditional values in Warsaw, Poland, before World War II. The journalist and novelist Elie Wiesel (1928–) produced *Night* (1958), which dealt with his personal experiences of Jews in concentration camps. Wiesel became chairman of the U.S. Holocaust Memorial Council in 1978 and was awarded the Congressional Gold Medal of Achievement in 1985 and the Nobel Peace Prize in 1986.

Canadian Novelists

Although Canadian writers explore many of the same themes as American writers, such as the plight of immigrants and aboriginals, there are, just as between the countries, some very stark differences.

Jewish American author Elie Wiesel was born in eastern Europe just prior to the rise of the Nazis in Germany. As a teenager during World War II (1939–1945), Wiesel was incarcerated in two concentration camps along with other members of his family, some of whom were killed. Since the end of the war Wiesel has written of his experiences in the camps and of the ethical and moral dilemmas of human nature. He has also been a tireless peace campaigner, speaking out against violence and injustice everywhere.

One such theme is identity: What does it mean to be Canadian? The answer is shaped by the geographical comparison Canadians must make with their American neighbors and the historical ties they have with their European founders, Great Britain and France.

Prior to the 20th century most English-language writing was usually about the pioneering spirit of European, particularly British, settlers conquering the vast landscape and indigenous peoples. In the early 20th century Canadian literature in English began to forge its own voice, and most of the works of this period dealt with the struggle of sustaining a rural life in the face of industrial, urban expansion. Stephen Leacock (1869–1944), who emerged during this period, is considered by some to be the founding father of Canadian letters and literature. A renowned humorist, his major works include *Literary Lapses* (1910) and *Nonsense Novels* (1911). In the late 20th century Robertson Davies (1913–2001) became the most famous Canadian writer. Some of his best-known works include the Deptford trilogy, published throughout the 1970s, and the Cornish trilogy, published in the 1980s.

Other important Canadian novelists include Alice Munro (1931–), esteemed author of *Lives of Girls and Women* (1971), *Who Do You Think You Are?* (1978), *The Progress of Love* (1986), and *Open Secrets* (1994), and Margaret Atwood (1939–), poet, novelist, and critic noted for her exploration of feminism and nationalism. Her novel *Handmaid's Tale* (1986) earned international fame.

See also

- Film (Volume 4)
- Music (Volume 7)

Lithuania is a small country on the coast of the Baltic Sea in north-central Europe. It borders Byelorussia, Latvia, Poland, and a small section of Russia. A Lithuanian-Polish Federation, formed in 1569, was conquered by Russia in 1795, and Lithuania remained under Russian control until it declared independence in 1918. It was annexed by the Soviet Union in 1940, becoming independent once again in 1991. Lithuanian immigrants have been arriving in North America from as early as the late 1600s.

Waves of Immigration

The first significant wave of Lithuanian immigration began in the 1860s, continuing through the early 20th century. It is estimated that around 300,000 Lithuanians arrived in the United States during this time and around another 9,000 in Canada, spurred on by famine, Russian repression, and the end of serfdom (working unpaid for a noble) in 1861. Many immigrants had little education, and few spoke English. The newcomers most often found employment in railroad construction, stockyards, meat-packing plants, and coal mines.

The majority of the new Lithuanian immigrants settled in smaller industrial towns in Massachusetts, Connecticut, and New Jersey, and near the coalfields of southern Illinois and the Shenandoah region of Pennsylvania. Almost 20 percent settled in Chicago. Although many of the earlier immigrants were not educated, they had established a small system of Lithuanian Catholic schools and a university by 1940.

Another large wave of immigration followed World War II (1939–1945) and the annexation of Lithuania by the Soviet Union. An estimated 30,000 Lithuanians entered the United States, settling in New York and California, as well as in states with established Lithuanian communities. Recent immigrants and second- and third-generation Lithuanian Americans do not have such strong cultural ties to their homeland as earlier immigrants. The later immigrants,

Some 10,000 Lithuanians march along Manhattan's Fifth Avenue for the Loyalty Day Parade on April 29, 1950. The banner reads "Thank you Uncle Sam, Lithuanian DPs." A Displaced Person (DP) is someone who has been forced to leave their home or homeland due to fear of persecution or deprivation of liberty.

however, were actively involved in working for Lithuania's independence from the Soviet Union and have remained very supportive of their homeland since 1991.

Lithuanian Culture

Initially, American Lithuanian communities were closely linked to those of Polish Americans. The preservation of Lithuanian culture has been important in both communities, due partly to the dominance of Poles in Lithuania and in the Lithuanian community. During the late 1900s, however, Lithuanians became more closely associated with the Latvian and Estonian communities, chiefly due to their common interest in independence for Baltic countries. These communities formed several organizations, including the Joint Baltic–American National Committee.

A number of Lithuanian Americans and Lithuanian Canadians have become involved in assisting Lithuania since it became independent in 1991. Several scholars and professionals have helped Lithuania improve its education and medical systems. Other immigrants have been active in fundraising and have engaged in political activity.

The Lithuanian American community has established several native-language newspapers. In addition, the Museum of Lithuanian Culture was established in Chicago in 1961 to increase ethnic awareness.

Notable Lithuanian Americans

Charles Bronson, actor.
Lane Bryant, fashion designer.
Dick Butkus, football player.
Ann Jillian, actress.
Johnny Unitas, football player.

See also

- Estonians (Volume 4)
- Latvians (Volume 6)
- Russians (Volume 9)
- World War II (Volume 10)

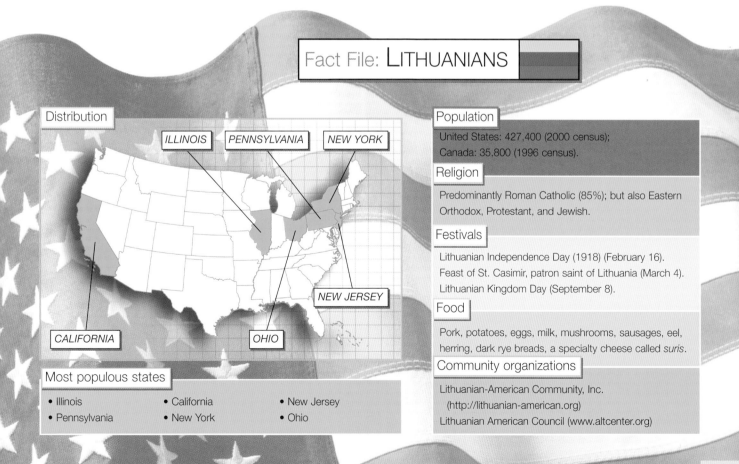

Fact File: LITHUANIANS

Distribution

ILLINOIS PENNSYLVANIA NEW YORK

NEW JERSEY

CALIFORNIA OHIO

Most populous states

- Illinois
- Pennsylvania
- California
- New York
- New Jersey
- Ohio

Population

United States: 427,400 (2000 census);
Canada: 35,800 (1996 census).

Religion

Predominantly Roman Catholic (85%); but also Eastern Orthodox, Protestant, and Jewish.

Festivals

Lithuanian Independence Day (1918) (February 16).
Feast of St. Casimir, patron saint of Lithuania (March 4).
Lithuanian Kingdom Day (September 8).

Food

Pork, potatoes, eggs, milk, mushrooms, sausages, eel, herring, dark rye breads, a specialty cheese called *suris*.

Community organizations

Lithuanian-American Community, Inc.
  (http://lithuanian-american.org)
Lithuanian American Council (www.altcenter.org)

Useful websites

Canadian constitutional documents
(www.solon.org/Constitutions/
Canada/English/index.html)
Canada Government Online
(www.gol-ged.gc.ca)
General Information
(www.library.ubc.ca/poli/cpwebr.
html)
Government of Canada
(http://canada.gc.ca)
National Library of Canada
(www.nlc-bnc.ca)
Prime minister's site
(http://pm.gc.ca)
Up-to-date government news
(www.journalismnet.com/canada/
parlt.htm)

In 1970 Pierre Laporte, a member of Quebec's cabinet, was killed by the Front de Libération du Québec (FLQ), a group demanding Quebec's independence from Canada. Laporte's was one of at least five violent deaths at the hands of the FLQ.

Canada is made up of 10 provinces (states) and three self-governing territories. Nunavut is the most recent of the territories, created in 1999 as a homeland for Canada's Inuits. Together the territories—Yukon, Northwest, and Nunavut—cover nearly 1.5 million square miles (3.9 million sq. km) and stretch well into the Arctic Circle. Because of the extreme wintry climate the population of the territories is sparse, yet all three have their own legislative assemblies. While none is controlled by the federal (national) government, all three territories elect representatives to the Canadian parliament.

The structure of the provincial governments is similar to that of Canada's federal government. At the head of each province sits a lieutenant governor who is appointed by the governor general and, like the governor general, is the representative of the British monarch. The real political power, however, lies with the provinces' legislative bodies, similar to U.S. state legislatures. Canadian legislatures are the law-making bodies for the provinces, made up of representatives elected by the provinces' citizens every five years or less. As in the parliament, the leader of the party with the majority of members in the assembly is the premier. He or she appoints other representatives, usually of the same party, to run the various provincial departments, which, again as at federal level, are known as the cabinet.

Provincial legislatures control a range of civil areas such as education, property laws, major health issues, and natural resources; legislatures can also set tax rates for provincewide projects. The provincial governments also oversee the provincial courts system (police, division, county, and superior courts), which includes the right of appeal up to Canada's federal supreme court.

Each province is made up of political divisions known as municipalities, similar to U.S. counties, each of which has its own elected body. Depending on its size and population, a municipality might include cities, towns, villages, and rural communities, again each with its own local governing body. There are around 4,600 different elected councils at municipal and local levels, and each of them is responsible for overseeing day-to-day issues such as local education, utilities, libraries, local services, as well as specific health and welfare concerns.

Local Representation of Multicultural Canada

Canada's large urban areas are highly cosmopolitan. Toronto is one of the most multicultural cities in the world—about 54 percent of its 4.6 million population are immigrants. While English is the city's dominant language, different ethnic groups speak dozens of other languages in their own homes and communities. Toronto's local council is the main governing and legislative body concerning local issues. It is made up of a mayor and 44 councillors. Today the council members come from a wide range of ethnic backgrounds and represent every side of Toronto's local issues. In areas where people from many cultures live and work side by side, it is easier for immigrants and those from minority groups to move into positions of power or government.

Top Immigrant Politicians

Since 1945 Canada has developed a positive stance on ethnic diversity. As a result, many of its influential politicians come from minority backgrounds. Ontario has led the way for members of immigrant groups to attain positions of power in local and national government: Leonard Braithwaite was the first black Canadian to be elected to a provincial legislature in 1963; Dr. Monestime Saint Firmin became the first black Canadian mayor in 1974; and in 1979 Lincoln Alexander served as the first black Canadian in the cabinet in his role as minister of labor. He went on to hold the position of lieutenant governor of Ontario between 1985 and 1991.

In 1995, 150,000 people in Montreal marched against independence for Quebec prior to a separatist referendum. In the referendum 50.6 percent of Quebecois voted against independence and 49.4 percent for.

Quebec Separatism

A notable issue in Canadian politics is the support within Quebec for self-governance or separatism (independence). Unlike the rest of Canada, Quebec is rooted in French rather than English culture. In the 1960s a militant political group, the Front de Libération du Québec (FLQ), called for the province to become an independent, French-speaking nation. In 1970 James Cross, the British trade commissioner, and Pierre Laporte, Quebec's minister of labor and immigration, were kidnapped by FLQ activists. Refusing to negotiate with the FLQ, Prime Minister Pierre Trudeau, with support from Quebec Premier Robert Bourassa, invoked the War Measures Act to send troops into Quebec and to suspend civil liberties. The next day Laporte was found murdered, but Cross was later released. Although the FLQ's actions were widely condemned, support for separatism has remained strong.

In 1976 the separatist Parti Québécois won control of the Quebec legislature. It adopted a law in 1977 to restrict English-language education, changed English place-names to French, and required public institutions to adopt French as the official language. However, in 1980, although the separatist party was still in power, voters rejected a referendum on independence. In 1995 Quebec rejected another referendum on secession, although this time the margin was much closer.

Women in local politics

For a period of time in 2000 women occupied five of the six senior political posts in the Yukon provincial government:
Judy Gingell, commissioner;
Louise Hardy, member of parliament;
Ione Christensen, senator;
Kathy Watson, mayor;
Pat Duncan, premier.

See also

- Local politics, U.S. (Volume 7)
- Multiculturalism (Volume 7)
- National politics, Canada (Volume 7)
- National politics, U.S. (Volume 7)
- Quebec separatism (Volume 9)

Glossary

affirmative action government programs to provide equal opportunities to minority groups.

alien a foreign-born resident who has not been naturalized and is still a subject or citizen of another country.

assimilation the process by which an individual or a minority group adopts the values and practices of the dominant culture and loses its own cultural distinctiveness.

asylum the legal status granted to a foreign individual who fears political persecution if he or she is forced to return home.

bilingualism the ability to speak fluently in two languages.

census a comprehensive survey of a population designed to gather basic demographic information. In the United States the census is carried out every 10 years.

citizen a native or foreign-born member of a country who has legal and political rights within that country.

colony a territory ruled by another country.

cultural mingling a process that occurs when two or more cultures come into contact and interact with one another.

cultural retention the process by which an immigrant group or individual retains elements of their native heritage in a new society.

deportation the legal removal of an immigrant from a country.

diaspora the historical dispersal of a group of people of similar origins from their homeland to many lands.

discrimination the unfair denial of equal rights or opportunities to a group or individual based on cultural, social, or racial differences.

emigrant a person who leaves his or her homeland to live in a foreign country.

emigration the movement of people from their homeland to another country.

emigré a person forced to emigrate for political reasons.

ethnic group a group sharing common origins and cultural similarities, such as beliefs, values, customs, and language, geography, kinship, or race.

ethnicity identification with and inclusion within an ethnic group.

exclusion act a law passed to refuse entry into the United States to a certain race or nationality.

ghetto an often deprived urban area occupied predominantly by members of a single race or ethnic group.

immigrant a person who moves to a country other than his or her homeland.

immigration the settlement of people in a country other than that in which they were born.

indigenous a term referring to the original inhabitants of a land or territory.

integration the mixing of different racial groups within a community.

melting pot a phrase coined by Jewish playwright Israel Zangwill to refer to America's multicultural society in the early 20th century.

middle class a socioeconomic class broadly defined as those with middle income working in mental rather than manual occupations.

migrant a term describing someone who regularly moves from one place to another, often for economic reasons.

migration the movement of people from one country to settle in another.

minority group a subgroup of society characterized by factors including race, religion, nationality, gender, or culture.

multiethnic a term meaning belonging not to one single racial or ethnic group but to two or more.

multiculturalism a positive attitude toward cultural diversity that supports the right of ethnic groups to maintain their cultural distinctiveness within the dominant culture.

nativism an anti-immigrant U.S. political tradition, popular in the 19th century, that valued "real" Americans and their attitudes over more recent immigrants.

naturalization the legal process by which a foreign person becomes a citizen of a country with the same rights as a native-born citizen.

pluralism the equal coexistence of diverse ethnic groups within a single society.

prejudice the holding of unfounded ideas about groups or individuals based on negative stereotypes.

quota (system) a limit on the number of immigrants from particular countries allowed into another.

race the classification of people based on genetic characteristics or common nationality, history, or experiences.

racism discrimination against others based on an assumption of one's own racial superiority.

refugee a term referring to a person who lives in a foreign country to escape persecution at home.

repatriation the forcible or voluntary return of immigrants to their country of origin.

segregation the discriminatory separation or isolation of ethnic, social, or religious groups, for example, in restricted areas such as ghettos.

slavery the ownership of human beings by others.

social mobility the movement of groups or individuals within the social hierachy.

stereotype a usually negative categorization of all individuals within a group based on a rigid and inflexible image of the characteristics of that group.

upper class the more affluent members of society, especially those who have great wealth or hold an esteemed position in society.

urban renewal the rebuilding of deteriorating city neighborhoods, often those that have become ghettos.

working class a social group made up broadly of people in manual occupations.

Ansari, Maboud. *The Making of the Iranian Community in America.* New York: Pardis Press, 1993.

Avery, Donald. *Reluctant Host: Canada's Response to Immigrant Workers 1896–1994.* Toronto: McClelland & Stewart, 1995.

Axtell, James. *Natives and Newcomers: The Cultural Origins of North America.* New York: Oxford University Press, 2000.

Barry, Brian M. *Culture and Equality: An Egalitarian Critique of Multiculturalism.* Cambridge, MA: Harvard University Press, 2001.

Bodnar, John. *The Transplanted: A History of Immigrants in Urban America (Interdisciplinary Studies in History).* Bloomington, IN: Indiana University Press, 1987.

Brown, Dee Alexander. *Bury My Heart at Wounded Knee: An Indian History of the American West.* New York: Henry Holt and Company, 2001 revised edition.

Capp, Diana White Horse. *Brother against Brother: America's New War over Land Rights.* Bellevue, WA: Merril Press, 2002.

Chavez, Leo R. *Shadowed Lives: Undocumented Immigrants in American Society.* Belmont, CA: Wadsworth Pub, 1997.

Ciongoli, A. Kenneth, and Jay Parini. *Passage to Liberty: The Story of Italian Immigration and the Rebirth of America.* New York: Regan Books, HarperCollins, 2002.

Connell-Szasz, Margaret (ed.). *Between Indian and White Worlds: The Cultural Broker.* Norman, OK: University of Oklahoma Press, 1994.

Daniel Tatum, Beverly. *Assimilation Blues: Black Families in a White Community.* Boulder, CO: Basic Books, 2000.

Dezell, Maureen. *Irish America: Coming into Clover.* New York: Doubleday, 2001.

Diner, Hasia R. *Jewish Americans: The Immigrant Experience.* Southport, CT: Hugh Lauter Levin Assoc., 2002.

Do, Hien Duc. *The Vietnamese Americans.* Westport, CT: Greenwood Press, 2000.

Flores, Juan. *Divided Borders: Essays on Puerto Rican Identity.* Houston, TX: Arte Publico Press, 1993.

Franklin, John Hope, and Alfred A. Moss. *From Slavery to Freedom: A History of African Americans.* New York: Alfred A. Knopf, 2000.

Frye Jacobson, Matthew. *Whiteness of a Different Color: European Immigrants and the Alchemy of Race.* Cambridge, MA: Harvard University Press, 1999.

Getis, Arthur, Judith Getis, and I. E. Quastler (eds.). *The United States and Canada: The Land and the People.* New York: McGraw-Hill, 2000.

Gonzalez, Juan. *Harvest of Empire: A History of Latinos in America.* New York: Viking Press, 2000.

Gonzalez-Pando, Miguel. *The Cuban Americans.* Westport, CT: Greenwood Press, 1998.

Govorchin, Gerald Gilbert. *From Russia to America with Love: A Study of the Russian Immigrants in the United States.* Pittsburgh, PA: Dorrance Publishing, 1993.

Grimes, Kimberly M. *Crossing Borders: Changing Social Identities in Southern Mexico.* Tucson, AZ: University of Arizona Press, 1998.

Hegi, Ursula. *Tearing the Silence: Being German in America.* New York: Simon & Schuster, 1997.

Hilfiker, David. *Urban Injustice: How Ghettos Happen.* New York: Seven Stories Press, 2002.

Horn, Michiel. *Becoming Canadian: Memoirs of an Invisible Immigrant.* Toronto: University of Toronto Press, 1997.

Inada, Lawson Fusao (ed.). *Only What We Could Carry: The Japanese American Internment Experience.* Berkeley, CA: Heyday Books, 2000.

Kelley, Ninette, and Michael J. Trebilcock. *The Making of the Mosaic: The History of Canadian Immigration Policy.* Toronto: University of Toronto Press, 1998.

Kelly, Paul. *Multiculturalism Reconsidered: Culture and Equality and Its Critics.* Cambridge, England: Polity Press, 2003.

Kibria, Nazli. *Becoming Asian American: Second-Generation Chinese and Korean American Identities.* Baltimore, MD: Johns Hopkins University Press, 2002.

Lehman, Jeffrey (ed.). *Gale Encyclopedia of Multicultural America.* Detroit, MI: Gale Research, Inc., 2000.

Miscevic, Dusanka, and Peter Kwong. *Chinese Americans: The Immigrant Experience.* Southport, CT: Hugh Lauter Levin Assoc., 2000.

Morton Coan, Peter. *Ellis Island Interviews: In Their Own Words.* New York: Facts on File, 1997.

Naff, Alixa. *The Arab Americans.* Broomall, PA: Chelsea House, 1998.

Portes, Alejandro, and Rubén G. Rumbaut (eds.). *Ethnicities: Children of Immigrants in America.* Los Angeles, CA: University of California Press, 2001.

Stoffman, Daniel. *Who Gets In: What's Wrong with Canada's Immigration Program—And How to Fix It.* Toronto: Macfarlane Walter & Ross, 2002.

Takaki, Ronald. *Strangers from a Different Shore: A History of Asian Americans.* New York: Back Bay Books, 1998.

Thernstrom, Stephan A., Ann Orlov, and Oscar Handlin (eds.). *Harvard Encyclopedia of American Ethnic Groups.* Cambridge, MA: Belknap Press, 1980.

Waldinger, Roger (ed.). *Strangers at the Gates: New Immigrants in Urban America.* Los Angeles, CA: University of California Press, 2001.

Winks, Robin W. *The Blacks in Canada: A History.* Montreal: McGill-Queens University Press, 1997.

Relevant websites are listed separately with each entry.

1492 Christopher Columbus sails to North America

1534 Jacques Cartier sails up the St. Lawrence River

1535 Spain establishes colonial government in Mexico

1607 Settlers from England establish a colony in Jamestown, Virginia

1776 Declaration of Independence

1795 Naturalization Act restricts U.S. citizenship to "free white males" who reside in the United States for five years

1798 Alien and Sedition Act allows deportation of "dangerous" foreigners. Naturalization Act increases the residency requirement to 14 years

1802 Congress reduces residency requirement from 14 years to four

1808 Congress bans importation of slaves

1819 Steerage Acts: data collected on immigration for the first time

1820 Chinese arrive in California

1830 Indian Removal Act forces Native Americans to give up their lands east of the Mississippi River

1834 Slavery abolished in British North America (Canada)

1840s Major immigration of Irish and Germans due to crop failures

1846 Mexican–American War starts

1848 Mexican–American War ends. United States purchases New Mexico, Arizona, California, Utah, Nevada, and Texas

1850 Fugitive Slave Act

1860s Mass immigration from Poland

1861 American Civil War begins

1862 American Homestead Act provides settlers with free land in the Midwest

1863 Emancipation Proclamation frees slaves in Union-held territory

1865 American Civil War ends; all slaves freed

1868 The Fourteenth Amendment endows slaves with citizenship. Japanese laborers arrive in Hawaii

1870 The Fifteenth Amendment: African American males given the right to vote

1880s Mass immigration from Italy. Civil unrest and economic instability throughout Russia

1882 Chinese Exclusion Act

1887 The Dawes Act dissolves many Indian reservations in United States

1890s Start of mass immigration of Ukrainians to Canada

1891 Polygamists, the sick, and those convicted of "moral turpitude" made ineligible for immigration

1892 Ellis Island opens

1896 Supreme Court rules that "separate but equal" facilities for blacks and whites are constitutional

1898 The Spanish–American War begins. U.S. acquisition of Puerto Rico and Guam

1900 Jones Act grants U.S. citizenship to Puerto Ricans

1901 Anarchist Exclusion Act

1907 Expatriation Act. "Gentleman's Agreement" curtails Japanese immigration

1910 Mexican Revolution begins: thousands of Mexicans flee to the United States

1917 The United States enters World War I

1918 World War I ends

1921 Quota Act restricts the immigration of southern and eastern Europeans

1924 Johnson–Reed Act reduces fixed quota to 2 percent of nationality groups. Oriental Exclusion Act limits immigration from East Asia. U.S. Border Control created

1929 Congress makes annual immigration quotas permanent

1930s Mass deportation of Mexicans during the Great Depression

1939 World War II begins

1940 Alien Registration Act requires registration and fingerprinting of aliens

1942 Japanese Americans moved to "relocation camps." Bracero Program allows Mexican laborers to work in the United States

1943 Magnuson Act repeals Chinese Exclusion Act of 1882

1945 World War II ends.

1948 Displaced Persons Act permits European war refugees entry to the United States

1950 Internal Security Act bars entry of communists to the United States. Korean War begins

1952 McCarran–Walter Immigration Act removes race as a basis for exclusion

1953 Congress amends the 1948 refugee policy to admit more refugees. Korean War ends

1954 U.S. Supreme Court rules that "separate but equal" educational facilities are unconstitutional. Operation Wetback: INS deports more than 3 million people of Mexican heritage

1959 Cuban revolution

1962 Amendments to Canada's Immigration Act eliminate racial and religious discrimination

1964 Civil Rights Acts

1965 Immigration Act ends quota system. Bracero Program ends. Vietnam War begins

1966 Cuban Refugee Act admits more than 400,000 people to the United States

1971 Canadian government officially endorses policy of multiculturalism

1975 Vietnam War ends: mass immigration from Vietnam

1980 Refugee Act: 10 million permanent immigrants are legally admitted to the United States

1986 The Immigration Reform and Control Act (IRCA) raises annual immigration ceiling to 540,000

1990 Immigration Act allows 700,000 immigrants per year into the United States

1991 Persian Gulf War

1995 Canada officially endorses policy of First Nations self-government

1996 Immigration Act mandates the building of fences on U.S.–Mexico border

2002 Department of Homeland Security established

2003 U.S. forces attack Iraq

Numbers in **bold** refer to volume numbers; those in *italics* refer to picture captions.

Acadians *see* Cajuns and Acadians
Acoma Pueblo **1**:*31*
actors and actresses
    English American **4**:13
    Italian American **6**:16
Adams, John **5**:*40*; **6**:54
Addams, Jane **6**:62
adobe architecture **1**:*31*, 32; **8**:6, *64*
affirmative action **9**:42, 68–69
Afghans **1**:*4*; **4**:7
African Americans **1**:*5–12*
    see also segregation and integration, slavery
    in broadcasting **2**:*8*
    cultural retention **3**:39
    discrimination against **5**:51
    families **4**:23
    festivals **1**:11; **2**:39; **4**:26
    housing **5**:18–19
    in industry and business **5**:48
    in literature **6**:64–65
    in local politics **7**:5
    in movies **4**:32
    and music **1**:*10, 12*; **4**:37
    newspapers and magazines **8**:23, *24*
    poverty **4**:61
    and Protestantism **9**:13–14
    return to Africa **9**:6; **10**:*60*
    shotgun houses **1**:*32*; **5**:18–19
    as slaves **1**:*5, 7–8*, 11; **2**:36, 38; **3**:5–6; **5**:31, 49; **6**:52; **8**:28
    social mobility **9**:66–67
    and sports **1**:12; **9**:69; **10**:14–15
    stereotypes **1**:*5*; **9**:*8*
    and World War I **10**:*55, 66*
    and World War II **10**:*55–56, 68, 69*
African Canadians **1**:*13–14*
Africans
    see also African Americans; African Canadians; East Africans; North Africans; South Africans; Southern Africans; West Africans
    crafts **3**:10
    folk medicine **5**:12, 13
    in Mexico **7**:18
    national loyalties **7**:38
    refugees **4**:6
    roots of American popular music **7**:34
Agassi, Andre **1**:*38*
agriculture **1**:*15–16*
    see also Bracero Program
    the Amish and **1**:*21*
    Belgians and **1**:61
    on the Great Plains **5**:49
    the Hutterites and **5**:26
    the Japanese and **6**:20
    Sikh farmers **9**:49
Alabama **10**:18
    Native Americans, Southeast **7**:68
Alamance, Battle of **9**:32
Alaska **10**:18
    Aleuts **1**:19–20
    border with Canada **3**:*18*
    and illegal immigration **3**:18
    Native Americans **4**:50; **7**:*44–45*, 66; **10**:34
    Russians **3**:7; **9**:24, *26*
Alaska Native Claims Settlement Act (1971) **7**:66; **10**:34
Albanians **1**:*17–18*
Alberta, English **2**:24
Albright, Madaleine **3**:*44*
Aleuts **1**:*19–20*; **7**:44, 45
    see also Inuit
Algerians **8**:32–33, *34*
Alien Act (1798) **8**:16
Alien and Sedition Acts (1798–1800) **1**:23, 24; **5**:*40*

Alien Enemies Act (1798) **8**:16
Aliens for Better Immigration Law **5**:16
Allende, Isabel **2**:51
Al Qaeda terrorist network **1**:4
America First Committee (AFC) **10**:67
American Indian Movement (AIM) **9**:54
American Indian Religious Freedom Act (1978) **8**:10
American Revolution (War of Independence) **1**:8; **3**:6, 17; **4**:11
    the French and **4**:44
    the Irish and **5**:65
    Loyalists **9**:15
    the Scotch-Irish and **9**:*30*, 33
American Samoans **8**:40
Amish **1**:*21–22*; **3**:52; **6**:42; **10**:25
    quilting **1**:*40*; **3**:10
Amity, Commerce and Navigation, Treaty of (1888) **7**:18
Anabaptists **1**:21; **7**:13; **9**:12
    see also Amish; Hutterites; Mennonites
Angel Island, California **5**:32, *34*
Anishinaabe *see* Chippewa
anti-immigrant discrimination *see* discrimination
anti-immigrant prejudice *see* prejudice
Apache **1**:*25–27*; **4**:23
Arab American Institute **8**:33
Arab Americans **1**:*28–30*
    see also Egyptians; Jordanians; Kuwaitis; Muslims; North Africans; Syrians
    newspapers **8**:24
Arapaho, Ghost Dance **4**:36
Arawaks **8**:66
architecture **1**:*31–32*
    see also housing
    adobe **1**:*31*, 32; **8**:6, *64*
    Belgian **1**:62
    Danish **3**:*45*
    Norwegian **8**:36
    Spanish **10**:*13*
    Ukrainian **10**:*44*
Argentines **1**:*33–35*
Arizona **10**:18
    Native Americans, Southwest **8**:5
Arkansas **10**:18
Arlington, Virginia, Bolivians **1**:66
Armenians **1**:*36–38*; **4**:5
Armstrong, Louis **1**:*12*
Arnaz, Desi, Jr. **3**:41
art **1**:*39–40*
    see also architecture; crafts; literature
    Javacheff (Christo) **2**:9
Articles of Confederation **6**:54
Asian American Citizenship Act (1946) **1**:41
Asian Indians **1**:*41–44*
    see also Sikhs; Sri Lankans
    dress **3**:52, 53
    employment of **5**:34
    Hinduism **5**:20; **9**:13
Asians **7**:31
    see also Central Asians; East Asians
    families **4**:22–23
    and local politics **7**:5
    refugees **4**:6–7
    repatriated **9**:15–16
    trades and professions **10**:36
    U.S. citizenship **9**:67
assimilation **1**:*45–49*; **3**:34; **6**:10
    see also Native Americans, assimilation
    Danish **3**:47
    English **4**:13
    French **4**:46
    Germans **4**:53–54
    Japanese **6**:24
    Mexican **7**:24
    Russians and **9**:27
    Salvadorans and **9**:28–29
    Southern Africans **10**:7

Swedish **10**:23
Association of MultiEthnic Americans (AMEA) **7**:33
Athabascans (Dene Nation) **7**:44, *45*
Audubon, John James **4**:44
Australians **1**:*50*
Austrians **1**:*51–52*
Austro-Hungarian Empire **1**:51
    Croatians **3**:14
    Czechs **3**:42
    Hungary **5**:21–23
    Romanians **9**:*21*
    Slovaks **9**:61
    Ukraine **10**:42
Azerbaijanis **1**:*53–54*
Azikiwe, Nnamdi **10**:63
Azores **8**:63
Aztecs **1**:*55–56*; **7**:17; **8**:6–7
    "writing" **6**:54

Back to Africa Movement **10**:60
Baer, Max **10**:*14*
Baha'is, in Iran **5**:60
Balanchine, George **4**:*51*
Balchen, Bernt **8**:38
Balkans **10**:8
Balkan Wars (1912–1913) **9**:*19*
Bangladeshis **1**:*57–58*
    see also Pakistanis
Bannock **7**:55, *56*
baptism, Mennonites and **7**:13
Baptists **9**:12
Barbadians **1**:*59–60*
barrio, el (Spanish Harlem) **8**:68, 69
Bartók, Béla **5**:23
Basques **7**:19; **10**:12
Batista, Fulgencio **3**:27
Battle y Ordóñez, José **10**:47
Beirut **6**:*50*
Belarusians **2**:12
Belgians **1**:*61–62*
Belizeans **1**:63
Bell, Alexander Graham **9**:*38*, 39
Beothuk people **7**:49
Berlin, New Hampshire **10**:65
Berry, Halle **4**:32
Bienville, Jean-Baptiste **4**:41
bilingualism **6**:45
Bill of Rights, Canadian (1960) **1**:43
Binational Border Safety Initiative **3**:26
Black Codes **9**:6
Blackfeet **1**:*64–65*; **7**:*49, 58, 59*
Black Panthers **3**:34
Black Power movement **10**:37
"blacks," definition **9**:7
Bloods and Crips (gangs) **3**:13
boat people **5**:7; **10**:*51*, 53
Bolden, Buddy **1**:12
Bolivians **1**:*66–67*
Borge, Victor **3**:*47*
Border Patrol, U.S. **3**:*19–24*
Borge, Victor **3**:*47*
Boskailo, Esad **1**:68
Bosnians **1**:*68–69*; **4**:6
Boston, Massachusetts
    Armenians **1**:37
    Brazilians **2**:5
    Irish Americans **5**:63
    Jews **6**:26
Bourbons **6**:10–12
Bracero Program **3**:23, 25; **7**:20, 23
Brazilians **2**:*4–6*
Britain *see* Great Britain
British Columbia
    African Canadians **1**:14
    English **2**:24
    Native Americans, Northwest Coast **7**:65
British Guiana **4**:*68*
British North America Act (1867) **2**:26, 29
broadcasting **2**:*7–8*; **6**:60
Bronck, Jonas **3**:45

Brown v. Board of Education (1954) **1**:10; **3**:66; **9**:9, 41, 67
Buddhism, Cambodians and **2**:*17*
buffalo **1**:64; **7**:58–60
Bulgarians **2**:*9–10*
Bureau of Indian Affairs (BIA) **3**:38; **8**:6, 10–11; **9**:17
Burmese **2**:11
Bury My Heart at Wounded Knee **6**:63–64
Bush, George W. **3**:19; **5**:15, 30, 39; **7**:*42*
Byelorussians **2**:12

Cabot, John **2**:25
Cabrillo, João Rodrigues **8**:61
Cajuns and Acadians **2**:*13–16*; **4**:44; **6**:55; **7**:35
California **10**:18
    African Americans **1**:6
    agriculture **1**:16; **4**:27; **5**:33; **9**:49
    Armenians **1**:37
    Asians and local politics **7**:5
    Bolivians **1**:67
    Cambodians **2**:18
    Chileans **2**:*51*
    Chinese **2**:52, *53, 54*, 59, 60; **9**:67
    Colombians **2**:*68*
    Costa Ricans **3**:9
    Cubans **3**:28
    Dutch **3**:*64*
    Finns **4**:*34*
    French **2**:*31*; **4**:45
    Gold Rush **1**:50; **4**:45
    Guatemalans **4**:*67*
    Hondurans **5**:17
    illegal immigrants **5**:30
    and intermarriage **5**:51
    Iranians **5**:60
    Japanese **6**:21
    Jews **6**:26
    Koreans **6**:34
    linguistic diversity **6**:45, 60
    Native Americans **7**:*46–48*; **8**:*13*
    Nicaraguans **8**:27
    reservations **7**:47, 48
    Pacific Islanders **8**:*41*
    Panamanians **8**:*48*
    Paraguayans **8**:*51*
    Peruvians **8**:*55*
    Spanish **10**:*13*
    Swiss **10**:26
    Vietnamese in **10**:51
Calusa **7**:67
Cambodians **2**:*17–18*; **5**:20
Canada
    border with Alaska **3**:*18*
    crossborder migration **3**:*17–20*; **5**:30
    Cuban trade with **3**:29
    Dominion of **2**:26
    emigration from **2**:22
    and the French **4**:*43*
    Great Seal of **2**:29
    immigration/emigration **2**:*19–22*; **5**:33
    and interfaith marriage **5**:53
    literacy in **6**:60
    local politics **6**:*68–69*
    multiculturalism **2**:21; **7**:30–31
    national politics **7**:*39–40*
    Nunavut **5**:58; **7**:31, 51; **8**:15
    oath of citizenship to **2**:19
    prime ministers **7**:*40*
    and religion **9**:11–12
    slavery **9**:58
    Ukrainians **10**:42
    and urban reform **10**:46
    and World Wars I and II **10**:56, 64, 68
Canadian Indian Act (1876) **7**:51
Canadians
    African **1**:*13–14*
    Armenian **1**:38
    Asian Indians **1**:41, 42, 43
    Australian **1**:50
    Austrians **1**:52
    Brazilians **2**:5

Cajuns **2:**14
Cambodians **2:**18
Chinese **2:**53
Chinese (overseas) **2:**59
Dutch **3:**57
Egyptians **3:**69
English **2:**23–29
Filipinos **4:**27, 28
Finns **4:**33, 34
French **2:**19, 21, 30–35; **4:**42
Germans **4:**54
Haida **5:**6
Hawaiians **5:**11
Hungarians **5:**22
Icelanders **5:**28
Indo-Fijians **8:**40–42
Inuit **5:**55
Iroquois Confederacy **6:**5
Israelis **6:**9
Italians **6:**10
Japanese **5:**33; **6:**21
Jews **6:**30
Koreans **6:**35
Libyans **8:**34
Lithuanians **6:**67
Maltese **7:**8
Mennonites **7:**14
Métis **7:**15–16
Mexicans **7:**20, 22, 23
Mormons **7:**29
Native Americans **7:**49–51
Norwegians **8:**36, 37
Pakistanis **8:**43, 44
Poles **8:**57
Portuguese **8:**62
Romanians **9:**22
Russians **9:**26–27
Sikhs **9:**49, 50
Slovaks **9:**59
South Africans **10:**4
Southern Africans **10:**6, 7
South Slavs **10:**9
Spanish **10:**10, 11, 13
Sri Lankans **10:**16
Swedes **10:**21
Swiss **10:**26
Syrians **10:**28
Thais **10:**31
Tlingits **10:**34
Trinidadians and Tobagonians **10:**38
Turkish **10:**40, 41
Ukrainian **10:**42–44
Vietnamese **10:**52, 54
Welsh **10:**59
West Africans **10:**61
Capone, Alphonse ("Al") **3:**12; **6:**15
Carey, Mariah **7:**32
Caribana festival **10:**38
Caribbean peoples **2:**36–37; **4:**7–8
 see also Barbadians; Cubans;
  Dominicans; Jamaicans; Puerto
  Ricans; Trinidadians and
  Tobagonians
Carignan, Jean **2:**32
Carmichael, Stokely **10:**37
Carnegie, Andrew **9:**39
carnivals, Caribbean **2:**36, 37
Carrere, Tia **4:**29
Carter, Jimmy **8:**47
Cartier, Jacques **2:**30; **4:**41
Carver, George Washington **1:**15
casinos **8:**6; **9:**18
Casquelourd, Malongo **2:**40
castes **1:**43
Catawba **7:**67, *68*
Catholicism *see* Roman Catholicism
Catlin, George **1:**64
Caucasians, North **2:**45
Central Africans **2:**38–41
Central Asians **2:**42–44
 see also Afghans; Armenians;
  Russians; Turks
Cernan, Eugene A. **9:**62

Chamorros **8:**40
Champlain, Samuel de **2:**13, 32; **4:**41, 49
Chanute, Octave **4:**45
Chaplin, Charlie **4:**31
Charter of Rights and Freedoms (1982: Canada) **7:**15
Chávez, César E. **1:***16*; **6:**40; **7:**24
Chávez, Hugo **10:***49*
Chechens **2:**45–46
Cherokee **2:**47–49; **7:***68*; **9:**6, 11
 language **2:**47–49; **6:***44*
 Trail of Tears **2:**49; **7:**67
Chiang Kai-shek **2:**60
Chicago, Illinois **2:**64; **4:**61; **10:**17, 18
 Arab Americans **1:**29
 black population **9:**42
 Bosnians **1:**68
 Brazilians **2:**5
 industry **5:**48, *49*
 Jews **6:**26
 Serbians **9:**46
 Swedes **10:**23, 24
Chicano Movement **7:**24
Chicanos **1:**24; **7:**24
Chickasaw **7:***68*, 69
children **1:**46–47
 see also education
Chileans **2:**50–51
Chinatowns **2:***52*; **3:**32, 41; **10:**36
Chinese **2:**52–57; **5:**32, 49
 businesses **10:**36
 discrimination against **9:**67
 and the family **4:**22
 illegal immigration via Mexico **3:**22
 immigrants detained **5:**32, *34*
 immigration suspended **1:**24; **2:**20, 54; **5:**32, 41, 42, 48
 medicine **5:***12*, 13
 in Mexico **7:**19
 national loyalties **7:**38
 New Year **2:**56–57; **3:**41; **4:**25
 Taiwanese **2:**59, 60–61
 "tongs" **3:**12, 35
Chinese Exclusion Act (1882) **1:**24; **5:**32, 41, 42; **9:**67
Chinese Immigration Service **3:**22
Chinese Six Companies **2:**55
Chinh, Kieu **2:**58
Chippewa (Ojibwa; Anishinabe) **2:**62–63; **7:**61; **9:**52
Chisholm, Shirley **1:**59
Choctaw **7:***68*, 69
Chopra, Deepak **1:***42*, *43*
Chrétien, Jean **7:**40
Christianity **9:**11–13
Chumash **7:**61
Ch'usok **6:**36
Cinco de Mayo festival **4:**26, 38; **7:**37
cities, U.S. **2:**64–65
citizenship **5:**40
 ceremonies **4:**53; **5:**32, *38*
 for Native Americans **9:**67
civil rights
 black **1:**9–10
 Mexican American **7:**24
 power movements **3:**35
Civil Rights Act (1964) **3:**53; **9:**68
Civil War, U.S. **2:**38; **5:**48; **9:**58; **10:**55, 58
 African Americans **1:**8; **9:***58*
Clarkson, Adrienne **2:**56
Clemente, Roberto **8:**68
Cleveland, Ohio, Slovenes **9:**64
clothes *see* dress and costume
Code Talkers, Navajo **6:**57
Cold War
 and Bulgarians **2:**9
 and ethnicity **2:**66
Cold/Hot Weather campaigns **3:**26
Cole, Nat King **3:**41
Cole, Thomas **1:**39, 40
Colombians **2:**67–69
colonial America **3:**4–6
Colorado **10:**18

color, definitions of **9:**7
Color Purple, The (Walker) **6:**64–65
Columbus, Christopher **9:**12
Comanche, and trickster figures **9:**11
communists
 communist witch-hunts **4:**32; **8:**18
 Red Scare and **6:**14–15; **8:**18
communities, immigrant **1:**46
Congress, U.S. **7:**42
 Cuban representatives **3:**29
Connecticut **10:**18
 Slovaks **9:**60
Constitution, U.S. **7:**41
Cooper, James Feinmore **6:**63
Coptic immigrants **3:**68
Cortés, Hernán **1:**56; **7:**18
Cosby, Bill **2:**8
Cossacks **3:**7
Costa Ricans **3:**8–9
costume *see* dress and costume
cotton **5:***48*, *49*; **9:**56
coureurs des bois **2:**32; **4:**43
cowboys **1:**16
crafts **1:**20; **3:**10–11; **10:**33
 see also art; stonecarving
Creeks *see* Seminole and Creeks
Creole **6:**43
crime
 ethnic **3:***12*–13
 on reservations **9:**18
 and the U.S.-Canadian law
  enforcement coalition **3:**17
Croatian Workers' Benefit Society **3:**14–16
Croatians **3:***14*–16; **10:**8–9
 Bosnian Croats **1:**68
Crockett, David "Davy" **9:**34
cross-border migration
 Canadian **3:**17–20; **5:**30
 Mexican **3:**21–26; **5:**30
Crow **5:***18*
Cubans **3:**27–29; **4:***8*, 22
Culloden, Battle of **9:**37
cultural borderlands **3:**30–32
cultural mingling **3:***31*–32, *33*–36
 English culture **4:***13*–14
 French culture **4:**46–47
cultural retention **1:**45–46; **3:**34, *37*–41
 see also language retention; national
  loyalties
 Arabic **1:**30
 Cajun **2:**16
 Caribbean **2:**37
 East African **3:**62
 German **4:**57
 Italian Mafia **3:**13
 Korean **6:**36
 Latvians **6:**49
 Native American **3:**38
 Pacific Islanders **8:**42
 Polish **8:**59
cultural tension **3:**34–35
Czechs **3:**42–44
 see also Slovaks

Dalai Lama **4:**7; **10:**32
dancing and dances
 Asian Indian **1:**41
 Costa Rican **3:**9
 Croatian **3:***16*
 flamenco **10:**13
 French influences **4:**47
 Greek **4:**64
 Hungarian **5:**25
 Irish **5:**65
 Jamaican **6:**19
 Métis **7:**15
 Mexican **7:**25
 Native American **7:**49, 57
 Pacific Islanders **8:**42
 Polynesian **5:**10
 salsa **3:**39
 Scottish **9:**35

step dancing **7:**16
 tango **1:**35
 Ukrainian **10:**42, 44
Danes **3:**45–48
Davies, Robertson **6:**65
Dawes, Henry L., and the Dawes Act **1:***46*; **8:**10
Day of the Dead **4:**24; **7:**37–38
Day of the Three Kings **1:**33
Day of Tradition **1:**33
Delaware **10:**18
 Native Americans, Northeast **7:**62
Dene Nation *see* Athabascans
Department of Indian Affairs **9:**17
deportation **5:***42*
 see also repatriation
Depression *see* Great Depression
Detroit, Michigan
 Arab Americans **1:**29
 Bangladeshis **1:**57, *58*
 Poles **8:**59
Dia de los Muertos, El, *see* Day of the
 Dead
diaspora
 Armenian **1:**36
 Jewish **6:**25–27
Diaz, Manny **7:**5
Diné College **8:**21
"Dirty War" **1:**33
discrimination, anti-immigrant **5:**32; **9:**40
 see also prejudice; segregation and
  integration
 against African Americans **5:**51
 against the Japanese **5:**31, 33; **6:**22,
  23; **8:***18*
 against Palestinians **8:**46
 and ethnic neighborhoods **9:**7–8
Displaced Persons Act (1948) **2:**66; **5:**43;
 9:23
District of Columbia **10:**18
 see also Washington, D.C.
Diwali **1:**41
Dominicans **3:**49–50
Dominion Land Act (1872) **2:**19; **10:**21
Dorsey, Thomas A. **1:**10
Douglas, Kirk **8:**52
Douglass, Frederick **6:**64; **9:**57
dress and costume **3:**51–53; **7:**37
 see also fashion
 Bavarian **4:**58
 Latvian **6:***48*
 Mayan **7:***10*, 11
 Mennonite **7:***13*
 Moroccan **8:***30*
 Native American **7:***48*, 64
 Norwegian **8:***39*
 Polish **8:***58*, 60
 Romany **5:***4*
 Spanish **10:***10*
 Vietnamese **10:***54*
 Zapotec **7:***19*
drug smuggling, cross-border **3:**20, 24;
 5:29
Du Bois, W.E.B. **3:**66; **6:**64
du Pont, E.I. **4:**41
Dutch, the **3:**5, 54–58
Duvalier, "Papa Doc" **5:**7

East Africans **3:**59–62; **5:**36
 see also Ethiopians; Somalians
East Asians
 see also Burmese; Laotians;
  Vietnamese
 refugees **4:**6–7
Ecuadoreans **3:**63–64
Edison, Thomas **9:**34, 39
education **3:**65–67
 see also literacy
 Asian Indians and **1:**44
 Central Africans and **2:**40
 Chinese and **2:**56
 cultural mingling in schools **3:**32
 desegregation in **9:**67, 68

Dominicans and **3:**50
East Africans and **3:**61
English and **4:**15
Finnish and **4:**35
Irish and **5:**68
Jews and **6:**30
Mennonites and **7:**14
multiculturalism and **7:**30
in the native language **6:**45
Pacific Islanders **8:**42
segregation in **3:**66; **6:**22; **9:**41, 43
Slovaks and **9:**61–62
and social mobility **9:**65, 67–68
Southern Africans and **10:**5
statistics **9:**67
Egyptians **1:**28–30; **3:***68–69*
1812, War of **1:**13; **3:***20*
Einstein, Albert **4:**53
El Salvador, people *see* Salvadorans
Ellis Island **1:**24, *49*; **3:***42*; **4:***19*; **5:***43*
deportations from **5:**42
medical examinations **5:**13, *42*
Emancipation Proclamation (1863) **1:**8, 11
emigrés and refugees **4:**4–8; **5:**34
anticommunist refugees **4:**8; **5:**39
Armenian **1:**36; **4:**5
Byelorussian **2:**12
Cambodian **2:**17
Cossack **3:**7
Latvian **6:**48–49
as returnees **9:**19
Southern African refugees **10:**7
Tibetan refugees **10:**32
to Canada **2:**21–22
Vietnamese refugees **10:**51–53
and World War II *see* World War II
employment *see* industry and employment
English **4:**9–15
in colonial America **3:**4–5; **4:**9–11
houses **3:**10
racial attitudes **9:**5–6, 8–9
sports **4:**15; **10:**14
English Only laws and movements **6:**54, 59
Erasmus, Georges **7:**51
Eritreans **3:**59
Eskimos **5:**54; **7:**44, *45*
Estonians **4:***16*
see also Latvians; Lithuanians
Ethiopians **3:**59; **4:***4, 17*
slaves from **3:***61*
ethnicity, multiple, *see* multiple ethnic origins
eugenics **9:**8
Europeans **4:**49
eastern European Jews **6:**28–29
family patterns **4:**20–21
and the frontier **4:**50
and medicine **5:**13–14
and music **7:**35
national loyalties **7:**37
trades and professions **10:**35–36
types of immigrant **4:**18–20
Evangeline (Longfellow) **2:**15
Executive Order 9981 **10:**56
explorers **4:**41, *44*, 50; **6:**11; **8:**61; **10:**10–12

Fair Housing Act (1968) **4:**61
Fairclough, Ellen **2:**21
family patterns **1:**49; **4:**18–23
Asian-Indian **1:**43
Cambodian **2:**18
East African **3:**62
and ghetto life **4:**61
Jewish **6:**30–31
Mexican **7:**24
North African **8:**35
Puerto Rican **8:**69
Romany **5:**4
Salvadoran **9:**29

Taiwanese **2:**61
farming *see* agriculture
fashion
African-American **1:**11
French **4:**47
federalism **7:**41
festivals **4:**24–26
Fifteenth Amendment **7:**41; **9:**66
Fifty-Sixers **5:**23
Fijians **8:**40
Filipinos **1:**16; **4:**23, *27–30*
film **4:***31–32*
emigrés in Hollywood **4:**5
Mexicans and **7:**25
names of movie stars **8:**52
Finns **4:**22, *33–35*
First Amendment **9:**12
First Nations people **7:**49–51
Fitzgerald, Ella **3:**41
Five Civilized Tribes **2:**47
Florida **10:**18
Argentines in **1:**34
Bolivians **1:**67
Chileans **2:**51
Colombians **2:**68
Costa Ricans **3:**9
Cubans **3:**28
Dominicans **3:**50
Dutch **3:**64
Finns **4:**34
French **2:**31
Guatemalans **4:**67
Hondurans **5:**17
Jews **6:**26
Native Americans, Southeast **7:**68
Nicaraguans **8:**27
Pacific Islanders **8:***41*
Panamanians **8:***48*
Paraguayans **8:**51
Peruvians **8:**55
Spanish **10:**12
Venezuelans **10:**50
folklore **4:***36–38*
food and drink **4:***39–40*
Argentinian **1:**34, 35
Caribbean **1:**60; **2:**37
Chinese **2:**53, 56; **3:**30
English Canadian **2:***23*, 24
"fast food" **4:**39, 40
French **4:**42, 46, 47
French Canadian **2:**31, 34, 35
"fusion food" **4:**40
German **4:**54, 58
kosher **3:***30*; **6:**28, 29
Native American **2:**48, 63
"soul food" **4:**40; **10:**62
Foran Act (1885) **6:**12–13
Forman, Milos **3:**44
Fort Nassau, New York **3:**54
Fort Wayne, Indiana **2:**11
Forty-Eighters **4:**55
Forty-Niners **5:**23
Fourteenth Amendment **7:**41; **9:**67
Franklin, Benjamin **6:**6; **9:**66
free speech, right of **7:**43
Freedom Riders **9:**41
French **1:**31; **4:***41–47*
French and Indian War **2:**32; **3:**17; **4:***44*
Battle of the Plains of Abraham (Battle of Quebec) **2:**32–33; **3:***17*
French Guyanese **4:***48*
French Revolution **4:**44
Front de Libération du Québec (FLQ) **6:**68, 69; **9:**4
frontier **4:**49–52; **5:**31–32, 49
Scotch-Irish and **9:**32
Fugitive Slave Bill (1850) **9:**58
fur traders **4:**43, 49; **7:**15; **8:**8

Gajdusek, Carleton Daniel **9:**61
Galarza, Ernesto **7:**23
Gallaudet, Thomas **4:**43
gangs **3:**13, 35

Garibaldi, Giuseppe **6:**10
Garifuna **5:**16, 17
Garvey, Marcus **9:**6; **10:**60
General Allotment Act (1887; Dawes Act) **1:***46*; **8:**10
Gentlemen's Agreement (1907) **6:**22, 35
Georgians **4:**51–52
Georgia **10:**18
Panamanians **8:***48*
Germans **4:**53–59; **5:**41, 47–48
Jews **6:**27–28
language **6:**54, 59, 60
"superior" race **9:**8–9
and World War I **10:**65
Germantown, Pennsylvania **4:**55, 56; **7:**13
Germany, Nazi **4:**5, 56; **5:**4; **6:***28*, 29
Geronimo **1:**27
Ghanaians **10:**63
ghettos **4:**60–61; **9:**42
Ghent, Treaty of (1814) **3:**20
Ghost Dance **4:**36
Giuliani, Rudolph **6:**13
Godfather, The (novel and movies) **3:**12; **4:***32*
Gold Rush, California **2:**50; **4:**45
Golem story **4:**37, 38
Gomes, Estévão **8:**61
Gompers, Samuel **6:**40
Gonzalez, Elian **3:**27
González, Rodolfo "Corky" **7:**24
Gore, Al **6:**42; **7:**42, *43*
Go Tell It on the Mountain (Baldwin) **6:**64
Graffenried, Christoph von **10:**25
Graham, Billy **9:**14
Great Awakenings **9:**12
Great Britain
see also English; Scottish; Welsh
immigration from **5:**41, 47
Great Depression **2:**27; **7:**23; **9:**16
Great Plains
farming of **5:**49
Native Americans **5:**18; **7:**58–60; **8:**13
Greeks **4:**62–64; **9:**19
see also Macedonians
Greeley, Horace **9:**34
Greenlanders **4:**65
Inuit **4:**65; **5:**56
Gretzky, Wayne **8:**60
Groulx, Lionel **9:**4
Grundtvig, Frederik Lange **3:**47
Guadalupe Hidalgo, Treaty of (1848) **7:**21
Guam **8:**40
Guarani **8:**50, 51
Guatemalans **4:**66–67
Mayans **4:**66; **7:**10, 11
Guess Who's Coming to Dinner (movie) **5:***52*
guild system **4:**57
Gulf War **5:**61
Gullah people **3:**10
Guyanese **4:**68–69
Guy, John **2:**25
Gypsies (Romany) **5:**4–5

Haida nation **5:**6
Haitians **1:**32; **5:**7–9; **6:***43*; **9:**20
Halloween **4:**24–25, 37
Hamilton, Alexander **9:**38–39
Handsome Lake **7:**63
Hanson, John **10:**21
Harambe **1:**11; **2:**39
Harlem, New York City **1:**59; **4:**60; **9:**42, 66
Spanish Harlem (*el barrio*) **8:**68
Harvard University **3:**65; **4:***14*, 15
Haudenosaunee **6:**4, 7
Hawaii **10:**18
see also Honolulu
Filipino workers **4:**28
Japanese **6:**21
Pacific Islanders **8:***41*

Hawaiians **5:***10–11*
language **5:**11; **6:**45, 58
literacy **6:**61
health and healing **4:**22; **5:***12–14*
Haitian **5:**9
medical examinations **5:**13, *42*
"hello girls" **10:**64
Helsinki Accord (1974–1975) **9:**23
Hendrix, Jimi **3:**35, 41
Herrera, Ramon **9:**69
Highland Clearances **9:**37
Highland Games **3:**53; **9:**39
Hinduism **1:***44*; **5:***20*; **9:**13
hip-hop culture **3:**36
Hispanic Americans (Latinos) **5:***15*
see also Belizeans; French Guyanese; Mexicans; Surinamese
architecture **1:**32
Argentines **1:***33–35*
art **1:**39
Bolivians **1:***66–67*
Brazilians **2:***4–6*
and broadcasting **2:**8
Chileans **2:***50–51*
Colombians **2:***67–69*
Costa Ricans **3:***8–9*
Cubans **3:***27–29*; **4:***8*, 22
Dominicans **3:***49–50*
economic and political migration **3:**25
Ecuadoreans **3:***63–64*
and the family **4:***21–22*
folklore **4:**38
Guatemalans **4:**66–67; **7:**10, 11
Guyanese **4:**68–69
Hondurans **5:***16–17*
and illegal immigration to Mexico **3:**24–25
language retention **6:**42
in local government **7:**5
music **7:**36
national loyalties **7:**37–38
newspapers **8:**24
Nicaraguans **8:***26–29*; **9:**20
Paraguayans **8:***50–51*
Puerto Ricans **6:**61; **7:**35; **8:***66–69*; **9:**66
refugees **4:**7–8
Salvadorans **9:**20, *28–29*
Venezuelans **10:***49–50*
Hmong **3:**10; **5:**35–36; **6:***46*, 47
Hoffa, James R. **6:**39
hogans **1:**31
Holland, Michigan **3:**57, *58*
Hollywood
communist witch-hunts **4:**32
emigrés in **4:**5
Holy Roman Empire **4:**55
Homeland Security, Department of **5:**30, 39
Homestead Act (1862) **1:**16; **3:**42, 45; **5:***49*; **8:**36; **10:**21
Hondurans **5:***16–17*
Hong Kong **2:**57, 59
Honolulu, Hawaii
Chinese **2:**53
Pacific Islanders **8:***41*
Hooks, Benjamin **2:**8
Hoover, Herbert **10:**25
Hopi Pueblo **8:**65
House Made of Dawn (Momaday) **7:**58
House Un-American Activities Committee **4:**32
housing **1:**31; **5:***18–20*
see also architecture
in the colonies **3:**6
in ghettos **4:**60, 61
Inuit **5:**54
log cabins **5:**19
Native-American **1:**26; **5:***18*; **6:**6; **7:**61, 63; **8:**6; **9:**44
public housing projects **4:**61; **5:***19–20*
segregation in **9:**42, 43
shotgun houses **1:**32; **5:***18–19*
tenements **4:**60; **5:***19*

Housing Act (1968) **9:**42
Housing and Urban Development, Department of 10:45
Houston, Sam **9:**34
Houston, Texas, Brazilians **2:**5
How the Other Half Lives (Riis) **2:**65
hoyaneh **6:**5–6
Huckleberry Finn (Twain) **6:**64
Hudson, Henry **3:**54
Hudson River School **1:**40
Hughes, Langston **6:**64
Huguenots **4:**43, 45, 47
Hull House **6:**62
Hungarian Revolution (1956) **5:**21, 22
Hungarians **5:**21–25
Hurons **4:**49; **7:**49, 61, 62, 63
Hussein, Saddam **5:**61, 62; **6:**37
Hutterites **3:**52; **5:**26–27; **6:**42

Icelanders **5:**28
Idaho **10:**18
    Native Americans, Columbia Plateau **7:**53
illegal immigration **5:**29–30, 34, 37, 44
    see also repatriation
    to Alaska **3:**18
    Bangladeshis **1:**57, 58
    Brazilian **2:**4, 6
    Colombians **2:**67
    Ecuadorians **3:**64
    from Canada **3:**19, 20
    from Mexico **3:**18, 21, 23–25; **5:**30, 34; **7:**21, 23
    "OTMs" (Other Than Mexicans) **3:**21
Illinois **4:**43; **10:**18
    Cubans **3:**28
    Czechs **3:**43
    Dutch **3:**64
    Guatemalans **4:**67
    Japanese **6:**21
    Jews **6:**26
    Koreans **6:**34
    Native Americans, Northeast **7:**62
    Paraguayans **8:**51
    Slovaks **9:**60
illnesses, and ethnicity **7:**33
immigrant experience **5:**31–36
Immigration Act
    of 1907 (U.S.) **3:**22–23
    of 1910 (Canada) **1:**14
    of 1917 (U.S.) **3:**23; **6:**61
    of 1924 (U.S.; National Origins Act; Johnson–Reed Act) **2:**40; **5:**43; **6:**12, 13; **8:**18
    of 1962 (Canada) **1:**43
    of 1965 (U.S.) **2:**40, 60; **4:**62; **6:**33, 35; **8:**43
    of 1990 (U.S.) **2:**40; **8:**43
Immigration and Nationality Act (1952) *see* McCarran-Walter Act
Immigration and Naturalization Service (INS) **5:**29, 37–39
immigration legislation, U.S. **5:**40–44
Immigration Reform and Control Act (1986) **5:**29–30, 44
Imperial Valley, California **1:**16; **4:**27
Independence, War of, *see* American Revolution
Indiana **10:**18
    Amish population **1:**22
Indian Citizenship Act (1924) **9:**67
Indian Defense Association **9:**9
Indian Defense League of America **9:**50
Indian Removal Act (1830) **2:**49; **4:**50; **9:**32
Indian Reorganization Act (1934) **7:**48; **9:**17
Indian Territory **2:**49; **7:**67, 69
Indians, Asian, *see* Asian Indians
Indo-Fijians **8:**40–42
Indochina, refugees from **4:**6
Indonesians **5:**45–46
Industrial Workers of the World **6:**39

industry and employment **5:**32–33, 47–49
    see also labor unions; trades and professions
    Italian **6:**13
    Jews **6:**30
    Korean **6:**35–36
    Native Americans and **6:**7; **8:**8
    Nigerians **8:**28
    Pacific Islanders **8:**42
    Puerto Ricans **8:**69
    railroad workers **2:**54; **4:**50; **9:**49
    Swedes **10:**21, 23
Inouye, Daniel Ken **6:**23
INS *see* Immigration and Naturalization Service
Intergovernmental Agencies for Refugees (IAR) **4:**4
intermarriage **4:**20, 23; **5:**50–53
    see also mestizos; Metis; multiple ethnic origins
Internet, languages and the **6:**41
Intifadah **6:**9
Inuit **4:**65; **5:**54–58; **7:**51
    see also Aleuts
Inupiats **7:**44
Inuvialuit **5:**57
Iowa **10:**18
    Czechs **3:**43
Iran–Contra affair **8:**27
Iranians **4:**7; **5:**59–60
    see also Kurds
Iraqis **1:**30; **4:**7; **5:**61–62
    see also Kurds
Irish **5:**32, 41, 47, 63–69
    employment **10:**35
    in the Mexican-American War **7:**19
    and politics **5:**68–69; **7:**4–5
    prejudice against **1:**23; **5:**41, 65; **8:**17
    repatriated **9:**15
    and World War I **10:**65
Iroquois Confederacy **4:**49; **6:**4–7; **7:**63; **9:**11
Ishi **7:**48
Israel **8:**45
    and Syria **10:**28
Israelis **6:**8–9
    see also Palestinians
Italians **3:**37; **4:**19; **6:**10–16; **10:**35
    and Catholicism **9:**12
    and the Mafia **3:**12–13; **4:**32
    temporary workers **9:**16
Italo-Turkish War **8:**33

Jackson, Andrew **9:**32
Jackson, Jesse **7:**5
Jamaicans **6:**17–19
James I, *king of England* **9:**30
Jamestown, Virginia **3:**4, 6; **4:**9, 55; **9:**12
    African Americans in **1:**5–7
    Poles in **8:**56
    slaves **9:**6, 55
Japan, and Mexico **7:**18
Japanese **5:**42; **6:**20–24
    discrimination against **1:**23; **5:**31, 33; **6:**22, 23; **8:**18
    dress **3:**51
    and the family **4:**22–23
    farmers **1:**16
    and music **7:**36
    and World War I **10:**55, 56
    and World War II **1:**23; **2:**20; **5:**31, 33; **6:**22, 23; **9:**20; **10:**55, 56, 67–68
Javacheff, Christo **2:**9
Javanese **5:**45
Jesuits **4:**44
Jews **1:**45; **3:**30; **6:**25–31
    and the Nazis **4:**5, 56; **6:**29; **10:**36
    folklore **4:**37, 38
    food and drink **3:**30; **6:**28, 29, 31
    from Israel **6:**8
    German **4:**56; **10:**35–36
    Jewish American writers **6:**65

marriage and weddings **4:**20
    in Mexico **7:**18
    moviemakers **4:**32
    New Year festival **4:**25; **6:**30
    Orthodox **9:**11, 13
    Polish **8:**56
    Reform **9:**13
    repatriated **9:**16
    as returnees **9:**19
    Russian/Soviet **5:**36; **7:**18; **9:**26, 27
    Sephardic **6:**27
Jim Crow laws **9:**40
Johnson, Lyndon B. **2:**40
Johnson–Reed Act *see* Immigration Act, of 1924
Johnston, George **10:**34
Jolliet, Louis **4:**41
Jolson, Al **4:**32; **9:**8
Jones, Marion **1:**63
Jordanians **6:**32
    see also Palestinians
Jordan, Michael **9:**68
Judaism **6:**25, 30
Jumper, Betty Mae **9:**45
Juneteenth **1:**11; **2:**39; **4:**26

Kachina festivals **8:**65
Kanjobal communities **4:**67
Kansas **10:**18
Kashmir **8:**44
Kawaiisu **7:**55, 56
Kee, Sing **10:**65
Kendall Township **8:**36
Kennedy, John F. **3:**68; **5:**66–67
Kentucky **10:**18
Kenya **3:**59, 60, 62
Kerouac, Jack **2:**35
Khannouchi, Khalid **8:**32
Khmer Rouge **2:**17, 18
Khomeini, Ruhollah **5:**60
Kikuyu people **3:**61
King, Martin Luther, Jr. **1:**9, 10; **9:**13, 41–42
King William's War **3:**17
Kingston, Maxine Hong **2:**55
Kissinger, Henry **4:**59
kivas **1:**31
Know-Nothings **8:**17
Koreans **5:**14; **6:**33–36; **10:**36
Korean War **6:**33, 35; **10:**56
Kosovo **1:**18; **9:**48
Ku Klux Klan **1:**8–9; **5:**51; **8:**18
Kurds **6:**37
Kuwaitis **6:**38
Kwanzaa **1:**11; **2:**39

labor unions **6:**39–40
Lafitte, Jean **2:**15
Land Claims Settlement Act (1971) **7:**45
land rights, native peoples and **4:**50; **5:**11; **6:**7; **7:**46; **8:**9–11
language
    see also language retention; linguistic groups
    American slang **5:**33
    Central African influence **2:**41
    Cherokee **2:**47–49; **6:**44
    and cultural mingling **3:**33
    Diné (Navajo) **8:**21
    Dutch **3:**57–58
    English **6:**61
    English Only laws and movements **6:**54, 59
    Filipino **5:**30
    French **5:**46; **6:**54, 60
    German **6:**54, 59, 60
    Hawaiian **5:**11; **6:**45, 58
    Hungarian **5:**22
    Icelandic **5:**28
    Inuit **5:**55
    Jewish **6:**26
    learning English **5:**33, 34–35; **6:**10, 27
    Maya **4:**67

Native Americans and **6:**42–45, 55–58, 61; **7:**47; **8:**14, 21, 65
Norwegian **8:**39
Pacific Islanders **8:**41
Serbo-Croatian **9:**48
Spanish **6:**55, 59, 60
language retention **6:**41–45
    by Aleuts **1:**20
    by Chechens **2:**45
    Cajun **2:**16
    Canadian bilingualism **2:**19, 21, 23–25
    Canadian English **2:**28–29
    languages spoken at home **6:**56
    Swahili **3:**59
Lansbury, Angela **4:**15
Laotians **6:**46–47
Laporte, Pierre **6:**68, 69; **9:**4
La Salle, Robert Cavelier de **4:**41
Last of the Mohicans, The (Cooper) **6:**63
Latin Americans *see* Hispanic Americans
Latinidad **3:**40
Latinismo **3:**40
Latvians **6:**48–49
    see also Estonians; Lithuanians
Laurel, Stan **4:**14
Leacock, Stephen **6:**65
Lebanese **1:**28; **6:**50–51
    see also Palestinians
Lee, Sammy **6:**36
Lee, Spike **4:**32
Leguizamo, John **2:**69
Lévesque, René **9:**4
Lewis and Clark expedition **4:**50
Lewis, John Llewellyn **10:**58
Lexington, Battle of **9:**30
Liberians **6:**52–53; **10:**60
Libyans **8:**33–34, 35
Lincoln, Abraham **8:**53; **9:**57–58; **10:**58
Lindbergh, Charles **10:**23
linguistic groups **6:**54–58
literacy **6:**59–61
    see also education
Literacy Test (1917) **5:**42
literature **6:**62–65
    Italian American writers **6:**16
    Jews and **6:**31
    Mexican **7:**25
Lithuanians **6:**66–67
    see also Estonians; Latvians
Little Bighorn, Battle of the **9:**17, 54
Little Italies **6:**10, 12; **10:**35
Little Norway homestead **8:**36
Little Odessa **9:**26
lobbying, political **7:**38
Lockerbie bombing **8:**33
Lodge, Henry Cabot **1:**24
Longfellow, H.W. **2:**15; **6:**62
"Long-House Religion" **7:**63
long houses **7:**61, 63; **10:**33
Long March **8:**21
Lopez, Jennifer **8:**69
Los Angeles, California **2:**65; **4:**61; **10:**18
    Argentines **1:**34
    Armenians **1:**36
    Brazilians **2:**5
    Cambodians **2:**18
    Chinatown **3:**32
    Chinese **2:**53
    Japanese **6:**20
    Jews **6:**26
    Koreans **6:**26
    Koreatown **6:**35, 36
    Pacific Islanders **8:**41
Lott, Trent **9:**42
Louisiana **4:**43; **10:**18
    see also New Orleans
    Cajuns and Acadians **2:**13–15, 16
    French **2:**31
Louisiana Purchase **3:**17; **4:**44; **5:**49; **6:**60
Louis, Joe **10:**14
luaus **5:**11
lunch counters, segregated **9:**41
Lutherans **10:**24

Luther, Martin 4:55, 58
Lyfoung, Nkauj'lis 6:46

MacDonalds 5:39
Macedonians 7:6
Mack, Charles 9:8
Madeira 8:63
Mafia 3:12–13; 4:32; 6:14, 15
magazines *see* newspapers and
magazines
Magyars 5:21
Maine 10:18
Canadian border 3:17–18
Native Americans, Northeast 7:62
Malaeska (dime novel) 6:62
Malaysians 7:7
see also Singaporeans
Malecite people 7:49
Maltese 7:8
Manhattan Island, purchase 3:54–56
Manifest Destiny 3:38; 4:49; 9:7
Mankiller, Wilma P. 2:49
Mao Tse-tung 2:60
maquiladoras 3:31
Marcantonio, Vito 6:16
Marcos, Sub-Commandante 7:11; 8:7
Mardi Gras 4:24, 47
Mariel Boat Lift 3:27
Marin, Rosario 9:69
Marquette, Jacques 4:41, 44
marriage(s)
see also intermarriage; war brides;
weddings
arranged 1:44, 58; 5:35; 8:43
Japanese picture brides 6:22
Mennonites and 7:13
Marsalis, Wynton 7:34
Marshall Plan 4:59
"Martin the Armenian" 1:37
Maryland 10:18
anti-Irish prejudice 1:23
Jews 6:26
Paraguayans 8:51
Masai people 3:62
Masaryk, Tomás 3:44; 9:59
Massachusetts 10:18
see also Boston; Provincetown
Cambodians 2:18
Chinese 2:53
Dominicans 3:50
Finns 4:34
French 2:31
Jews 6:26
Massachusetts Bay Colony 9:12, 15
Plymouth colony 3:4
Mauritians 7:9
Mayans 4:66; 7:10–11, 17; 8:6–7
and Zapatistas 8:7, 15
Mayflower Compact 3:4
Mayflower (ship) 3:4
McCarran–Walter Act (Immigration
and Naturalization/Nationality Act;
1952) 2:54, 66; 3:23; 4:28; 5:43–44;
6:23; 10:5
McCarthy, Joseph 8:18
media, mass
see also broadcasting; newspapers
and cultural mingling 3:34
medical examinations, for immigrants
5:13, 42
medicine
see also health and healing
alternative 1:43
medicine men (shamans) 1:64; 5:56;
10:33
Meech Lake Accord (1987) 9:4
Mehta, Zubin 5:53
Melanesia 8:40
Mellon, Andrew 9:34
"melting pot" 1:48
see also cultural mingling
Mennonites 7:13–14; 10:25
and cross-cultural dating 5:52

dress 3:52
Paraguayan 8:51
Menominee 7:12
Mescalero 1:26
mestizos 7:17, 67; 8:12; 9:5
Mestrovic, Ivan 3:16
Métis 4:43; 5:50; 7:15–16, 51; 9:6
Mexicali, Chinese in 7:19
Mexican-American War 7:21
and the Irish 7:19
Mexican Farm Labor Program
Agreement 3:23
Mexican Revolution 7:22
Mexicans 7:21–25
see also Aztecs; Chicanos; Mayans;
Mexico
in the Alaskan fishing industry 3:18
crafts 3:10
discrimination against 1:24
families 4:21–22
festivals 4:24, 26, 38
folklore 4:38
labor unions 6:40
language 6:59; 7:24; 8:14
stereotypes 9:9
trades and professions 10:36
Zoot-Suit Riots 9:7, 8; 10:69
Mexico
border 3:21, 22, 23–24, 26, 30–31;
5:30; 7:21
cultural borderlands 3:30–31
emigration from 3:21–26; 7:20
illegal immigration from 3:18, 21,
23–25; 5:30, 34; 7:21, 23
immigration 7:17–20
literacy in 6:61
Native Americans 8:6–7, 12
oil reserves 3:25
and World War I 10:65
Zapatista movement 7:11; 8:7, 15
Miami, Florida
Brazilians 2:5
Cubans 3:27, 29
Jamaicans 6:18
Jews 6:26
Nicaraguans 8:26
Michigan 10:18
Armenians 1:37
Bulgarians 2:9
Finns 4:34
French 2:31
Native Americans, Northeast 7:62
Micmac 2:15; 7:49, 61
Micronesia 8:40
middlemen (sojourners) 9:16
Middle Passage 9:56
Midsommarfest 10:24
migrant workers *see* workers, migrant
military, the, *see* war and military service
Miller, Dorie 10:67
Mills, Billy 9:54
Milosevich, Slobodan 9:46, 48
mining towns 5:19
Minnesota 10:18
Czechs 3:43
Finns 4:34
Native Americans, Northeast 7:62
Minority Health, Office of 4:22
minstrel shows 9:8
Minuit, Peter 3:54–55
Miranda, Carmen 8:61
miscegenation 5:51
Mississippi 10:18
Native Americans, Southeast 7:68
Missouri 10:18
Mixtecs 7:17; 8:6–7
mobility, and cultural mingling 3:34
Mohawks 6:7; 7:61, 62; 8:8
moieties 7:46
mojados 3:25
Molly Maguires 5:65
Momaday, N. Scott 7:58
Mongolians 7:26

Montana 10:18
Blackfeet 1:64, 65
Native Americans, Columbia
Plateau 7:53
Native Americans, Great Plains 7:59
Montcalm, Louis-Joseph de 3:17
Montenegrins 7:27
see also Serbians
Montezuma II 1:56
Montreal
African Canadians 1:14
Chinese population 2:52
cultural events 2:35
Monument Valley, Arizona 8:19
Moody, Dwight Lyman 9:10
Moran, George 9:8
Moreira, Airto 2:6
Mormons 4:50; 5:28; 7:28–29; 9:14
and cross-cultural dating 5:52
polygamy 4:21
Moroccans 8:30–32, 34
Morrill Act (1862) 3:66
Morrison, Toni 6:64
Morse, Samuel F.B. 8:17; 9:34
mosques 1:28
mountain men 4:50
Mukherjee, Bharati 6:64
multiculturalism 1:48–49; 7:30–31
Canadian 2:21; 7:30–31
Multiculturalism Act (1988; Canada) 7:31
multiple ethnic origins 7:32–33
see also intermarriage
Munro, Alice 6:65
murals 4:61; 7:25
music 7:34–36
and African-Americans 1:10, 12; 4:37
bluegrass 7:35
blues 7:34
Cajun 2:15, 16
Caribbean 6:19
classical 7:35
Conjunto 3:31
and cultural mingling 7:35–36
Ecuadorian 3:64
folk 7:35
French-Canadian 2:35
gamelan orchestras 5:45
gospel 1:10; 7:34
Hispanic 7:36
Hutterites and 5:26
Inuit 5:57
Irish 5:69
Jamaican 6:19
jazz 1:12; 2:6, 40; 7:34
"Latino" 3:40
mariachi 7:36
Métis 7:16
Mexican 7:25, 36
Native American 7:36
norteño 7:36
Peruvian 8:54, 55
politicized 3:36
polka 8:60; 9:63
pop (popular) 4:14; 7:34
Puerto Rican 8:69
rap 1:12; 3:36
rock-'n'-roll 7:34, 36
Romanian 9:23
salsa 7:36
swing 7:34
zydeco 7:35
Muslims 1:28, 29; 7:30
Azerbaijani 1:53
dress 3:53
Iranian 5:60
Iraqi 5:61
Pakistani 8:43
polygamy 4:21
and racism 9:9
Shi'ite 5:60, 61
Sunni 5:61
Turkish 10:39, 41
Mutombo, Dikembe 2:41

Nader, Ralph 1:30
names
personal 8:52–53
place 6:56; 10:10
Napoleonic Wars 2:26
Narváez, Pánfilo de 7:18
Nast, Thomas 8:16
National Association for Bilingual
Education (NABE) 6:42
National Association for the
Advancement of Colored People
(NAACP) 1:9–10; 9:9
National Broadcast Company (NBC) 2:7
National Chicano Survey (NCS) 6:59–60
National Farm Workers Association 6:40
National Football League 9:69
National Health and Social Living
Survey (1994) 5:53
national loyalties 7:37–38
see also cultural retention; language
retention
National Origins Quota Act (1920) 2:40
National Origins Quota Act (1924) *see*
Immigration Act, of 1924
Nation of Islam 1:11
Native American Association 8:17
Native American Church 7:60
Native American Religious Freedom
Act (1978) 1:27
Native Americans
see also Aleuts; Apache; Aztecs;
Blackfeet; Cherokee; Chippewa;
Inuit; Mayans; native peoples;
Navajo; Pueblo; reservation
system; Tlingits
in Alaska 4:50; 7:44–45
architecture 1:31
art 1:39
assimilation 1:46, 47–48; 3:30, 38, 51,
67; 6:61; 7:48; 8:10; 9:17
in California 7:46–48; 8:13
in Canada 7:49–51
in colonial America 3:4
Columbia Plateau 7:52–54; 8:13
crafts 3:10–11
criminal gangs 3:13
dancing 7:49
displaced 4:50
dress 3:51
education 3:67
the English and 9:6
European culture imposed on 3:30
families 4:23
farmers 1:15
folklore 4:36–37
Great Basin 7:55–57; 8:13
Great Plains 5:18; 7:58–60; 8:13
housing 1:26; 5:18; 6:6; 7:61, 63; 8:6;
9:44
intermarriage 5:50
languages 6:42–45, 55–58; 7:47
in literature 6:63–64
medicine and healing 5:13
Menominee 7:12
Mexico's 8:6–7, 12
music 7:36
newspapers 8:23
Northeast (Woodland peoples)
7:61–63; 8:13
Northwest Coast 7:64–66; 8:9, 13
population statistics 8:15
religions 7:63; 9:11
sacred lands 8:9, 10
segregation 9:41
Southeast 7:67–69; 8:13, 14
Southwest and Mexico 8:4–7, 13
Spanish conquistadors and 9:5
and state names 6:56
Sun Dance 7:59
taiko 7:36
treaties with 4:49
as U.S. citizens 9:67
women as religious leaders 9:11

workers **6**:*8*; **8**:*8*
and World War I **10**:55
and World War II **10**:68–69
native peoples **8**:*12–15*
and land rights **4**:50; **5**:11; **6**:7; **7**:46;
8:9–11
nativism **8**:*16–18*
see also prejudice, anti-immigrant
Naturalization Act
of 1798 **5**:40; **8**:16
of 1870 **6**:20–22
of 1906 **5**:38
Navajo **1**:31; **4**:23; **8**:*4, 14, 19–21*
Code Talkers **6**:57; **10**:69
language revitalization **6**:44
and oil reserves **8**:6
and the Rainbow Bridge **8**:*10*
reservation (Navajo Nation) **8**:*19*; **9**:18
rugmaking **3**:*11*
Navajo–U.S. Treaty (1868) **8**:21
neighborhoods, ethnic **1**:46
Nebraska **10**:18
Czechs **3**:*43*
Native Americans, Great Plains **7**:59
Nevada **10**:18
New Amsterdam **3**:5, *54*
New Brunswick, French Canadians **2**:*31*
New Deal **8**:21
New England **3**:5, 17
French Canadians **2**:30, 33, *34*
houses **1**:31; **5**:18
Newfoundland, English **2**:*24*
New France **2**:32, 33; **3**:17; **4**:43; **9**:4
New Glarus, Wisconsin **10**:26
New Hampshire **10**:18
New Jersey **10**:18
Arab Americans **1**:*29*
Chileans **2**:*51*
Chinese **2**:53
Colombians **2**:*68*
Costa Ricans **3**:*9*
Cubans **3**:*28*
Dominicans **3**:*50*
Dutch **3**:*64*
Hondurans **5**:*17*
Jews **6**:26
Koreans **6**:*34*
Nicaraguans **8**:*27*
Paraguayans **8**:*51*
Peruvians **8**:*55*
Slovaks **9**:*60*
New Mexico **10**:18
Native Americans, Southwest **8**:5
New Orleans, Louisiana **4**:43, *45*
Congo Square **2**:*40*
Jazz Festival **1**:*11*
Mardi Gras **4**:24, *47*
Newroz **6**:*37*
New Spain **7**:18; **8**:4
newspapers and magazines **8**:*22–24*
Newton, Huey P. **3**:*34*
New York City **2**:*64–65*
see also Ellis Island
African street vendors **10**:*62*
Annual Turkish Day parade **2**:42, *44*
Arab Americans **1**:*29*
Argentines **1**:*34*
Armenians **1**:*37*
Bangladeshis **1**:57, *58*
Barbadians **1**:*59*
Brazilians **2**:4, 5, *6*
Chinese **2**:53
cultural mingling **3**:*31–32*
Dutch **3**:*54–56*
Ecuadoreans **3**:*63*
ghettos **4**:*60*, 61
Haitians **5**:*7–9*
Jamaicans **6**:*18*
Jews **6**:25, 26, *29*
Koreans **6**:*34*
Little Italy **6**:*12*
marriages outside ethnic groups **4**:*20*

Philippine Day Parade **4**:*30*
Puerto Ricans **8**:68
St. Patrick's Day Parade **4**:25; **7**:37
tenements **5**:*19*
Thanksgiving Day Parade **4**:26
New York State **10**:18
African Americans **1**:6
Bolivians **1**:*67*
Chileans **2**:*51*
Chinese **2**:52, 53
Colombians **2**:*68*
Costa Ricans **3**:*9*
Cubans **3**:*28*
Czechs **3**:*43*
Dominicans **3**:*50*
Dutch **3**:*64*
Finns **4**:*34*
French **2**:*31*
Guatemalans **4**:*67*
Hondurans **5**:*17*
Jews **6**:26
Koreans **6**:*34*
Native Americans, Northeast **7**:*62*
Nicaraguans **8**:*27*
Pacific Islanders **8**:*41*
Panamanians **8**:*48*
Paraguayans **8**:*51*
Peruvians **8**:*55*
Slovaks **9**:*60*
New Zealanders **8**:*25*
Nez Percé **7**:54; **8**:14
Nguyen, Dat **10**:*54*
Nicaraguans **8**:*26–29*; **9**:20
Nikolski **1**:*19*
Nisei Week celebrations **6**:20, 24
Nkrumah, Kwame **10**:*63*
Noriega, Manuel **8**:47
North Africans **8**:*30–35*
North Carolina **10**:18
Cherokee **2**:*49*
Native Americans, Southeast **7**:*68*
North Dakota **10**:18
Native Americans, Great Plains **7**:59
North Star, Project **3**:17
Northwest Passage **5**:*56–57*
Norwegians **8**:*36–39*
Nova Scotia **2**:25, 32
English **2**:*24*
expulsion of Acadians from **2**:*13*
Native Americans, Northeast **7**:*62*
Noxche (language) **2**:*45*
Nunavut **5**:58; **7**:31, 51; **8**:15

Oakland, California, Chinese **2**:53
Oath of Allegiance, U.S. **5**:38
occupations *see* industry and
employment
Ohio **10**:18
Amish population **1**:*22*
Czechs **3**:*43*
Finns **4**:*34*
Slovaks **9**:*60*
oil reserves **3**:25; **8**:6
Ojibwa *see* Chippewa
Oklahoma **10**:18
Cherokee **2**:*49*
Native Americans, Great Plains **7**:59
Native Americans, Southeast **7**:*68*
Oktoberfest **4**:54, *58*
Old Spanish Days fiesta **6**:*55*
Oliver, Frank **2**:20
Olmecs **7**:17; **8**:6, *7*
Ontario
see also Ottawa
African Canadians in **1**:*14*
English **2**:*24*
Estonians in **4**:*16*
French Canadians **2**:*31*
Germans in **4**:*58*
Jews **6**:26
Native Americans, Northeast **7**:*62*
On the Road (Kerouac) **2**:*35*
Opium War **2**:54, *58*

Oregon **10**:18
Finns **4**:*34*
Native Americans, Columbia
Plateau **7**:53
Pacific Islanders **8**:*41*
Treaty of (1846) **3**:18
Orthodox Church **4**:64; **9**:23
Greek **4**:64
in Protestant societies **9**:14
Russian **9**:26
Serbian **9**:46, 48
Ukrainian **4**:5, 6
Osceola **9**:*44*, 45
Otavalo, Ecuador **3**:*63*, 64
Otay Mesa crossing **3**:26
"OTMs" illegal immigrants **3**:21
Ottawa, Ontario
Parliament Building **7**:*39*
tulip festival **3**:58
Ottoman Empire **1**:36; **8**:33; **10**:39

Pacific Islanders **8**:*40–42*
see also Hawaiians; New Zealanders;
Papua New Guineans
padrones **6**:*12–13*
Pahlavi, Mohammed Reza **5**:59
Paige, Rod **6**:*61*
paintings *see* art
Paiute **7**:55, 56
Pakistanis **8**:*43–44*
see also Bangladeshis
Palestinians **1**:28; **8**:*45–46*
see also Israelis
Palmer raids **8**:17
Panama Canal Treaty (1978) **8**:47
Panamanians **8**:*47–48*
Papineau, Louis-Joseph **9**:4
Papua New Guineans **8**:*49*
Paraguayans **8**:*50–51*
Parks, Rosa **9**:*40*, 41
Parti Québécois **6**:69
Pashtuns **1**:4
Peace Arch State Park **3**:20
Peace Maker **6**:6
Pearl Harbor **5**:31; **6**:22; **10**:67
Pella, Iowa **3**:56, *57–58*
Peña, Guillermo Gómez **3**:31
Penn, William **4**:*11*, 55; **9**:12
Pennsylvania **4**:11; **9**:12; **10**:18, 58
see also Philadelphia
Amish population **1**:*22*
Dominicans **3**:*50*
Jews **6**:26
Slovaks **9**:*60*
Pennsylvania Dutch (Pennsylvania
Germans) **1**:22
Pennsylvania Gazette, The **8**:22
Pensionado Act (1903) **4**:28
Perez, Hugo **9**:28
Persian Gulf War **5**:61
personal names **8**:*52–53*
Peruvians **8**:*54–55*
petroglyphs **1**:*39*
Peyotism **7**:60
Philadelphia, Pennsylvania **4**:*11*
Jews **6**:26
Mummers' Parade **4**:24
philanthropy, Greeks and **4**:62
Philippines, immigrants from, *see*
Filipinos
Pilgrims, the **3**:4; **4**:9
piñatas **4**:*38*
Pinkster Day **2**:38
Pinochet, Augusto **2**:50, 51
Pittsburgh Agreement (1918) **9**:*59–61*
Pittsburgh, Pennsylvania, Croatians
3:14, 15
Plains of Abraham, Battle of the **2**:32, 33
Plains people *see* Great Plains, Native
Americans
Plantation of Ulster **9**:30
plantations **1**:*7*; **3**:5; **5**:*48, 49*; **9**:*56–57*
in Hawaii **4**:28

Plessy v. Ferguson (1896) **1**:9; **3**:66; **9**:7
pluralism **9**:10
Plymouth, Massachusetts, colony **3**:4
poetry **6**:*62–63*
Poitier, Sidney **4**:32; **5**:52
Poland, origins of **8**:56
Poles **8**:*56–60*
politics
English **4**:15
Guatemalan **4**:*67*
Guyanese **4**:*68*
Haitian **5**:9
Hondurans **5**:16
the Irish and **5**:68–69; **7**:*4–5*
the Italians and **6**:15–16
Jamaican **6**:17
Jews and **6**:31
Koreans and **6**:36
and lobbying **7**:38
local politics (Canada) **6**:*68–69*
local politics (U.S.) **7**:*4–5*
"machine" **7**:4
national politics (Canada) **7**:*39–40*
national politics (U.S.) **7**:*41–43*
Polish **8**:60
and religion **7**:42; **9**:10
Polonia **8**:58
polygamy **4**:21; **7**:28, 29
Polynesia **8**:40
Portuguese **8**:*61–63*
Potawatomi **8**:9
potlatch **5**:6; **7**:66
costume **7**:*64*
poverty **4**:61
Powell, Colin **1**:5
Prado, Perez Pantalon **3**:*36*
prejudice, anti-immigrant **1**:*23–24*; **3**:26;
5:32
see also discrimination; nativism;
racial prejudice and racial theories
against Arabs **1**:28
against Filipinos **4**:29
against Germans **6**:59; **8**:16, 18
against the Irish **1**:23; **5**:41, 65; **8**:17
against Italians **6**:*14*
against Japanese **6**:20–22
against Poles **8**:59
against Ukrainians **10**:42
against Vietnamese **10**:53
in Canada **2**:21
and diseases of immigrants **5**:13
post-September 11, 2001 **5**:33
Presbyterians **9**:12
presidents, U.S. **7**:42
Presley, Elvis **7**:*36*
Prohibition **3**:23
Prohibition of the Slave Trade Act
(1808) **10**:60
Proposition 187 **1**:24; **3**:26
Protestantism **9**:10, *12–13*
evangelical Protestants **9**:14
Germans and **4**:55, 57
Provincetown, Massachusetts,
Portuguese **8**:63
Prudhomme, Paul **2**:16
Pueblo **8**:6, 9, *64–65*
Ancestral **8**:64
Pueblo Revolt **8**:64; **9**:11
pueblos **1**:31
Puente, Tito **3**:41
Puerto Ricans **8**:*66–69*; **9**:66
language **6**:61; **8**:67
and *West Side Story* **7**:35
Pulitzer, Joseph **8**:23
Puritans **7**:42; **9**:12
Puzo, Mario **6**:64

Qaddafi, Muammar al- **8**:33
Quakers **3**:5; **9**:12
see also Germantown
colony for **4**:11
Quebec
cultural events **2**:35

English Canadians **2**:25
French Canadians **2**:*19*, 21, *31*, 33
language **2**:*19*; **7**:31; **9**:4
separatism **2**:34; **6**:55, *69*; **7**:40; **9**:*4*
and World War I **10**:64
Quebec City **2**:25, *26*, 35
Battle of the Plains of Abraham
(Battle of Quebec) **2**:*32–33*; **3**:*17*
early French colony **4**:*43*
Quebecois **6**:54, 55
Quiet Revolution **9**:4
quilting **1**:*40*; **3**:10
quince, los **1**:33
quinceaño **3**:63
quota system **5**:38–39, 43, 44

race riots
Chicago (1919) **2**:64
Los Angeles (1965) **2**:65
racial equality, in the military **10**:56
racial prejudice and racial theories **9**:*5–9*
see also Manifest Destiny; prejudice,
anti-immigrant
radio *see* broadcasting
railroad workers **2**:*54*; **4**:50; **9**:*49*; **10**:35
Rainbow Bridge, Utah **8**:9, *10*
Rakcheyeva, Sabina **1**:53
Ramadan **1**:57
rancherias **7**:48
Rastafarians **6**:*19*
Reagan, Ronald **5**:*44*, *67*; **8**:26
recessions, economic **5**:33
Reconstruction **1**:8
redemptioners **4**:56
Red River Resistance **7**:15
Red Scare **6**:14–15; **8**:18
Reform, War of the **7**:22
Refugee Escape Act (1960) **10**:8
Refugee Relief Act (1953) **2**:66; **10**:8
refugees *see* emigrés and refugees
refusniks **9**:27
Regulator movement **9**:32
religion **9**:*10–14*
see also Amish; Hutterites; Judaism;
Mormons; Muslims; Orthodox
Church; Protestantism; Roman
Catholicism
of African Americans **1**:11; **10**:63
Anabaptists **1**:21
of Arab Americans **1**:29
Buddhism **2**:17
Bulgarian Orthodox church **2**:9–10
and cultural mingling **3**:33
dress of religious groups **3**:51–53
of English Canadians **2**:28
Gypsies and **5**:4–5
Hawaiian **5**:11
Hinduism **1**:*44*; **5**:20; **9**:*13*
Hungarian **5**:24
and interfaith marriage **5**:52–53
Irish **5**:67–68
of the Iroquois **6**:6–7; **9**:11
Native American **6**:6–7; **7**:63; **9**:11
Peyotism **7**:60
politics and **7**:42; **9**:10
United Church of Canada **2**:28
repatriation **9**:*15–16*
see also deportation; returnees
reservation system **8**:6, 10; **9**:*17–18*
Apache reservations **1**:27
Blackfoot reservations **1**:65
California reservations **7**:*47*, 48
fractionalization **8**:10
Menominee reservations **7**:12
Sioux reservations **9**:52, 54
returnees **9**:*19–20*
see also repatriation
Revolutionary War *see* American
Revolution
Rhode Island **10**:18
Dominicans **3**:*50*
Ribaut, Jean **4**:*41*
Riel, Louis **7**:16; **9**:6

Rights and Freedoms, Charter of (1982;
Canada) **7**:31
Riis, Jacob **2**:65
Ringgold, Faith **1**:40
Roanoke Island **3**:4
rock carvings **1**:*39*
Rohani, Shardad **5**:59
Rojas, Arnold J. **6**:64
Roman Catholicism
see also Jesuits
Cajuns and **2**:16
Croatians and **3**:16
early **9**:12
and education **3**:65
the French and **4**:44–45
French Canadians and **2**:33
Maltese and **7**:8
Mexicans and **7**:*24*
Poles and **8**:59
in Protestant societies **9**:14
Salvadorans and **9**:29
Samuel Morse and **8**:17
Romanians **9**:*21–23*
Romany, (Gypsies) **5**:*4–5*
Roosevelt, Franklin D. **2**:7
Roosevelt, Theodore **6**:22
rootwork **5**:12
Rosh Hashanah **4**:25
Rush-Bagot Agreement (1818) **3**:*20*
Russians **9**:*24–27*
see also Cossacks; Soviet Union; Tatars
cultural identity **5**:36
Jews **5**:36; **7**:18; **9**:26
and Latvia **6**:49
Mennonites **7**:13

Sacco, Nicola **6**:14–15
Sadlirmiut **5**:57
Said, Edward **8**:46
St. Louis, Missouri, Pacific Islanders **8**:*41*
St. Lucy's Day **10**:24
St. Patrick's Day **5**:69
parades **4**:*25*; **5**:*69*; **7**:37
Saipan **8**:40
Salish **9**:41
Salt Lake City, Utah **7**:28
Pacific Islanders **8**:*41*
Salvadorans **9**:20, *28–29*
Samoans **8**:40
Sandanistas **8**:26, 27
San Diego, California, Pacific Islanders
8:*41*
San Francisco, California **10**:17
African Cultural Festival **2**:41
Brazilians **2**:5
Chinatown **2**:52; **3**:*41*
Chinese **2**:53
Jews **6**:26
Koreans **6**:34
Pacific Islanders **8**:*41*
Santa Rosa, California, Scottish
Highland Games **5**:53
Saroyan, William **6**:64
Saund, Dilip Singh **9**:50
Schneider, Rob **4**:29
schools *see* education
Schwarzenegger, Arnold **1**:*51*
Scotch-Irish **9**:*30–34*
Scots **9**:35–39
Ulster *see* Scotch-Irish
Scottish Enlightenment **9**:38
sculptures **5**:*58*; **8**:28
Seattle, Washington, Pacific Islanders
8:*41*
Second Fort Laramie Treaty (1868) **9**:*17*,
54
Second Seminole War **9**:*44*
segregation and integration **1**:9, 10;
9:*40–43*
see also discrimination, anti-
immigrant; prejudice, anti-
immigrant
and housing **4**:61

Japanese **6**:20, 22, 23
segregation in education **3**:66; **6**:22;
9:41, 43
Seles, Monica **9**:48
Seminole and Creeks **9**:*44–45*
Creeks **7**:67, *68*, 69; **9**:*44–45*
Seminole **7**:67, *68*, 69; **9**:*45*
"separate-but-equal" doctrine **9**:7,
40–41
September 11, 2001, attacks **1**:4, 28; **3**:*20*;
5:40, *5*:44; **10**:9
and the "axis of evil" **5**:60, 62
and border defenses **3**:19
and illegal immigrants **5**:30
immigrant harassment and dress **3**:53
and the INS **5**:39
prejudice and suspicion after **5**:33;
8:35
Sequoyah **2**:47
Serbians **9**:*46–48*; **10**:9
see also Montenegrins
Serbs, Bosnian **1**:68
Serra, Junipero **10**:*12*, *13*
servants, indentured **1**:7; **9**:37, 38
shamans *see* medicine men
sharecroppers **1**:*15*, 16
Sharif, Omar **3**:*68*
Shaw, Bernard **2**:8
Shining Path **8**:54
shoe game, **8**:21
Shoshone **7**:55, *56*, 57; **8**:*11*
Sidhu, Sanjiv **5**:35
Sifton, Clifford **2**:20
"signcutting" **3**:19
Sikhs **3**:53; **9**:*49–50*
Sinatra, Frank **6**:15
Singaporeans **9**:51
see also Malaysians
Singer, Isaac Bashevis **6**:65
Sioux **5**:18; **7**:58, 60; **8**:15; **9**:17, *52–54*
slavery **9**:6–7, *55–58*
African-American slaves **1**:5, *7–8*, 11;
2:36, 38; **3**:*5–6*; **5**:31, 49; **6**:52; **8**:28
African-Canadian slaves **1**:13–14
East African **3**:*61–62*
freed **6**:52
names **8**:52, *53*
reparations for **9**:57
schools for ex-slaves **3**:66
slaves in the Caribbean **2**:36; **9**:55
slaves from the Caribbean **5**:31
Slavs **4**:*21*
South **10**:*8–9*
Slovaks **9**:59–62
see also Czechs
Slovenes **9**:*63–64*
Smart Border Declaration **3**:19
Smith, Alfred E. **7**:*4*
Smith, Jedediah **4**:50
Smith, Joseph **7**:28, 29
social mobility, and race **9**:65–69
sodbusters **5**:18
sod shanties **5**:18
sojourners (middlemen) **9**:16
Solidarity **8**:60
Solvang, California **3**:*45*, 48
Somalians **3**:59; **4**:6
Soriano, Edward **4**:27
South Africans **10**:4
South Carolina **10**:17, 18
anti-Irish prejudice **1**:23
Gullah people **3**:*10*
Native Americans, Southeast **7**:*68*
slaves **3**:5–6
South Dakota **10**:18
Native Americans, Great Plains **7**:*59*
Tribal Land Enterprise **8**:11
Wounded Knee **8**:15
Southern Africans **10**:*5–7*
South Slavs **10**:*8–9*
Soviet Union
see also Cold War; Russians
and Central Asia **2**:44

invasion of Chechnya **2**:45
Jews from **6**:29
Soyinka, Wole **8**:29
Spanish-American War **8**:*66*
Spanish Civil War **7**:19–20
Spanish Harlem (*el barrio*) **8**:68
Spanish language **6**:55, 59, 60; **7**:24
Spanish people **10**:*10–13*
see also Basques
early conquest by **7**:10, *18*; **8**:4, 64,
65; **9**:*5*
and Mexico **7**:17, 19–20
and racism **9**:5
sports **10**:*14–15*
African Americans and **1**:12; **9**:69;
10:14–15
baseball **8**:68; **9**:69; **10**:14–15
basketball **10**:14, 15
boxing **9**:69; **10**:*14*, 15
cricket **6**:19; **10**:14
diving **6**:36
English **4**:15; **10**:14
football **9**:69; **10**:15, 54
golf **7**:33
hockey **8**:*60*; **10**:14
hurling **5**:68
integration in **9**:*43*
lacrosse (stick ball) **7**:69
running **8**:32; **9**:*54*
soccer **6**:53; **9**:28; **10**:47
Thai boxing **10**:30, 31
Sri Lankans **10**:16
states, U.S. **10**:*17–18*
names **6**:56
Steerage Acts (1819) **5**:41
stereotypes **9**:9
of African-Americans **1**:5; **9**:*8*, 9
of Italian Americans **6**:14–15
of Poles **8**:59
of Russians **9**:27
Steuben Day parades **4**:58
stonecarving **3**:11; **5**:*58*
stores and storekeepers **10**:*19*
Stowe, Harriet Beecher **10**:58
Uncle Tom's Cabin **6**:62, 64; **10**:58
Strauss, Levi **5**:49
Stroessner Matiauda, Alfredo **8**:51
Stuyvesant, Peter **3**:56
subway, in Chicago **1**:*68*
summer camps **1**:*48*
Sun Dance **7**:59
Supreme Court
Canadian **7**:40
U.S. **7**:41, 43
Supreme Order of the Star-Spangled
Banner (Know-Nothings) **8**:17
Surinamese **10**:20
Susan Constant (ship) **4**:*9*
Suu Kyi, Aung San **2**:11
Swahili **3**:59
Swedes **5**:19; **9**:15; **10**:*21–24*
Swiss **10**:*25–26*
Syrians **10**:*27–28*
see also Palestinians

Taiwanese **2**:59, *60–61*
Tajikistan **2**:42
Taliban **1**:4
tamales **3**:8, 9
Tammany Hall **5**:65
Tan, Amy **6**:64
tango **1**:*35*
Tanzania **3**:60, 61
Tatars (Tartars) **10**:29
Taylor, Charles **6**:52
Tekesta **7**:67
television *see* broadcasting
Temporary Protective Status (TPS), for
Liberians **6**:53
tenements **4**:60; **5**:*19*
Tennessee **10**:18
Native Americans, Southeast **7**:*68*
tepees **5**:*18*; **6**:6

terrorist attacks
  see also September 11, 2001, attacks
  Libya and **8**:33, 35
Tesla, Nikola **3**:*16*
Teton (Lakota) **9**:52
Texas **10**:18
  Cajuns **2**:15
  Chileans **2**:*51*
  Chinese **2**:53
  Colombians **2**:*68*
  Costa Ricans **3**:9
  Cubans **3**:28
  Czechs **3**:*43*
  French **2**:*31*
  Guatemalans **4**:*67*
  Hondurans **5**:*17*
  Houston **9**:34
  Koreans **6**:34
  Nicaraguans **8**:27
  Pacific Islanders **8**:*41*
  Panamanians **8**:48
  Paraguayans **8**:*51*
Texas Rangers **3**:21
Tex-Mex **3**:31; **4**:*40*; **7**:24
textile industry **5**:47
Thais **10**:30–*31*
Thanksgiving Day **4**:26, *40*
Tibetans **4**:7; **10**:32
  Dalai Lama **4**:7; **10**:32
Tijerina, Reies López **7**:24
Tippu Tip **3**:61–*62*
Tlingits **5**:6; **7**:*64, 65*; **10**:*33–34*
tobacco **5**:*48*
To Kill a Mockingbird (Lee) **6**:64
Toltecs **7**:*17*; **8**:6, *7*
Tongans **8**:40
"tongs," Chinese **3**:12, 35
Toronto
  African Canadians **1**:14
  Africans **9**:66
  Bosnians in **1**:69
  Chinese population **2**:59
  English **2**:*24*
  Jews **6**:26
  local council **6**:68–69
  totem poles **7**:*44, 64, 66*
trades and professions **3**:10; **10**:*35–36*
  see also industry and employment
  Venezuelans **10**:50
Trail of Tears **2**:49; **7**:67, 69; **9**:32
transnationalism **7**:38
Tresca, Carlo **6**:14
Trianon, Treaty of (1920) **5**:23
Tribal Land Enterprise **8**:11
Trinidadians and Tobagonians **10**:*37–38*
Trudeau, Pierre **2**:20, 21
Trujillo, Rafael **3**:49
Truman, Harry S. **5**:39; **6**:23; **8**:*68*
Tsimshians **7**:*44*
Tunisians **8**:*34*–35
Turchaninov, Ivan (John Turchin) **3**:7

Turkey, *see also* Armenians
Turks **10**:*39–41*
  see also Kurds
Turner, Nat **1**:8; **9**:57
Tuskegee Airmen **10**:68
Twenty Years at Hull House (Addams)
  6:*62*

Uganda **3**:61
Ukrainians **10**:*42–44*
  see also Cossacks
  in Canada **2**:20
  Orthodox Church **4**:*5, 6*
  and World War I **10**:42, 64
Ulster Scots *see* Scotch-Irish
Unangans *see* Aleuts
Uncle Tom's Cabin (Stowe) **6**:62, 64; **10**:58
Underground Railroad **1**:13; **9**:58
unions, labor **6**:39–40
United Church of Canada **2**:28
United Farm Workers union (UFW) **1**:16
United Irishmen **9**:32
United Nations, and refugees **4**:4
Universal Negro Improvement
  Association (UNIA) **9**:6
universities **3**:65; **5**:68
urban deprivation *see* ghettos
urban reform and race **10**:*45–46*
Uruguayans **10**:*47–48*
Utah **10**:18
  Mormons **7**:28
  Pacific Islanders **8**:*41*
  Serbians **9**:48
Ute **7**:55, *56, 57*

Vancouver
  African Canadians **1**:14
  Chinese population **2**:52, 59
Vanzetti, Bartolomeo **6**:14–15
Vatra **1**:18
Vegreville, Alberta **10**:42
Velvet Revolution **9**:61
Venezuelans **10**:*49–50*
Vermont **10**:18
Vesterheim Museum, Iowa **8**:39
Vietnamese **4**:6; **10**:*51–54*
  Hmong women **3**:10
Vietnam War **6**:46
View of Boston (Cole) **1**:*39*
Virginia **10**:18
  Bolivians **1**:*67*
  Native Americans, Northeast **7**:*62*
  Pacific Islanders **8**:*41*
  Paraguayans **8**:*51*
  Peruvians **8**:*55*
voodoo **5**:7, 9, 13

Waldensians **6**:11
Walesa, Lech **8**:60
Walters, Barbara **2**:8
war and military service **5**:47; **10**:*55–56*

war brides **1**:50; **4**:*12*; **10**:57
War Measures Act (1914) **10**:64
"war on terror" **1**:4
War Relocation Authority **1**:23
Warrior gangs **3**:13
Washington, Booker T. **3**:66
Washington, D.C.
  Bolivians **1**:*67*
  Brazilians **2**:5
  Jews **6**:26
  Koreans **6**:34
  March on **1**:9; **9**:41
  National Cathedral **3**:11
  White House **7**:41
Washington State **10**:18
  Finns **4**:34
  Japanese **6**:21
  Native Americans, Columbia
    Plateau **7**:53
  Native Americans, Northwest Coast
    7:65
  Pacific Islanders **8**:*41*
Washoe **7**:55, 56, 57
Weah, George **6**:53
weaving **8**:*21*
  basket **7**:55
weddings
  see also marriage(s)
  Greek **4**:64
  Hindu **1**:44
  intermarriage **5**:51
  Jewish **4**:*20*
  Pacific Islanders **8**:42
Welch, Raquel **1**:*66*
Welsh **10**:*58–59*
West Africans **10**:*60–63*
  see also Liberians
Western Samoa **8**:*40*
West Side Story (movie) **7**:35
Wetback, Operation **3**:25
West Virginia **10**:18
whaling **5**:57
White Buffalo, The (Catlin) **1**:*64*
Whitman, Walt **6**:63
Wiesel, Elie **6**:65
wikiups **8**:6
Wilson, Woodrow **9**:33
Wisconsin **10**:18
  Czechs **3**:43
  Little Norway homestead **8**:*36*
  Native Americans, Northeast **7**:*62*
Witherspoon, John **9**:38
Wolfe, James **2**:25; **3**:*17*
Woman Warrior, The (Kingston) **2**:55
women
  see also war brides
  Hmong **6**:47
  Iroquois **6**:4–5; **9**:11
  in local politics **6**:69
  Macedonian **7**:6
  Native American **7**:60; **9**:11

West African **10**:60
Woods, Tiger **7**:33
workers, migrant **3**:25
  Bracero Program **3**:23, 25; **7**:20
  Filipino **4**:*27*, 28
  Puerto Rican **8**:*68*
Work, Hubert **8**:9
World War I **10**:*64–66*
  African Americans and **10**:55, *66*
  and Armenians **1**:36, 38
  and black migration **1**:9; **9**:42
  Canada's role in **10**:56, 64
  German Americans and **10**:65
  and the German language **6**:59
  Irish Americans and **10**:65
  Native Americans and **10**:55
  and Turks **10**:39
  and Ukrainians **10**:42, 64
World War II **10**:*67–69*
  see also war brides
  African Americans **10**:55–56, 68, 69
  British evacuees to Canada **2**:26
  Canadians in **2**:29; **10**:68
  Estonian refugees **4**:16
  and the French **4**:45
  and the Italians **6**:15
  and the Japanese **1**:23; **2**:20; **5**:31, 33;
    6:22, 23, 56; **9**:20
  and Jews **4**:56
  Mexican Americans in **10**:56, 67
  and Mexican labor **7**:20, 23
  Native Americans and **6**:57; **10**:*68–69*
  Navajo Code Talkers **6**:57
  Pearl Harbor **5**:*31*
  Poles and **8**:56–58
  postwar war brides **1**:50; **2**:26–27
  refugees from **2**:66; **4**:16; **5**:39, 43;
    6:29, 48–49; **8**:58; **9**:26–27, 63
  Russian refugees **9**:26–27
  and South Slavs **10**:8
  and Ukrainians **10**:*42–43*
Wounded Knee **8**:15; **9**:54
Wright, Carroll D. **2**:33
Wyoming **10**:18
  Native Americans, Great Plains **7**:59

Yahi culture **7**:48
Yakima **7**:*54*
Yugoslavia, Federal Republic of **7**:27
  see also Montenegrins; Serbians
Yugoslavia, former
  see also Macedonians
  national loyalty to **7**:38
  refugees from **4**:6
Yupiks **7**:44

Zapatista movement **7**:11; **8**:7, 15
Zapotecs **7**:17, *19*; **8**:6–7
Zimmerman Telegram **10**:65
Zonians **8**:47, 48
Zoot-Suit Riots **9**:7, 8; **10**:69

Picture credits

Front cover: Corbis: Lee Snider; **background image: Corbis:** Bettmann. **Corbis**: 8, 40, 57, 59; Morton Beebe 19; Nathan Benn 4, 31; Bettmann 12, 14, 16, 28, 36, 43, 62, 66; Natalie Fobes 58; Owen Franken 50; Anne Griffiths Belt 44; Illustrated American 52; Nazima Kowall 7; Earl + Nazima Kowall 69; Richards T. Nowitz 29; Steve Raymer 46; Brain Smith 68; Lee Snider 41; Joseph Sohm/Chromo Sohm Inc 20; Ted Spiegel 17; Nik Wheeler 35, 55; Michael S. Yamashita 24; **Getty Images**: 6, 27, 30, 48, 54, 64; Archive Photos 23; Ewing Galloway 25; Lawrence Migdale 45; Nancy R. Schiff 65; **Library of Congress**: 10, 39; **National Archives of Canada**: 22; **Photos12.com**: Collection Cinema 63; **Rex Features**: Mirek Towski 13; **Robert Hunt Library**: 15, 33, 67; **Topham**: Image Works 42, 60; **U.S. Department of Education**: 61.